An Expat's Guide to Costa Rica

Costa Rica Immigration, Housing and Living Options, Work & Business, Family & Education, Retirement, Relocation Tips, Taxes & Banking, Essential Expat Guide and Much More!

By Tess Downey

Foreword

Costa Rica is a small country located in the Caribbean particularly in Central America. The country is usually characterized by the friendliness and hospitality qualities of its people, and is also a well – known tourist destination filled with spectacular natural sceneries. It is one of the great places where tourists and locals alike can find great quantities of natural destinations which many of them not even known by the locals themselves. Their capital city is in San Jose is filled with lots of tourist attractions that future expats like you can truly enjoy.

Near the capital city is where you can visit national parks and see different natural sceneries like volcanoes with amazing formations, beaches, rivers and evergreen forests. If you choose to live in the pacific side of the country, you can witness two of the most important national areas in the country; one of which is described by Nat Geo as one of the richest place biologically speaking in the whole world. The country also boasts a biosphere reserved which was also declared as the "heritage of humanity." If eco – tourism is what you want to experience during your stay, then you've come to the right place as most natural destinations here are untouched by modern developments.

Costa Rica is a natural country with certainly no 'artificial ingredients.' If you wanted to get to know nature, experience the warmth of its people, and live the excitement then this is the place for you! This book will provide you with plenty of information about how to settle in Costa Rica as an expat, the amazing opportunities you can take advantage of, and how you can make the most out of this national treasure located in the heart of Central America.

Table of Contents

Pura Vida Costa Rica!

Costa Rica is a place filled with vibrant people, unique culture, and natural sceneries. And since this country is located in Central America, you can expect it to have a very relax way of living just like in most countries located in the continent. Aside from lushes natural reserve, the country also boasts the larges wetland in Central America which is perfect if you're an expat looking for an adventure of if you're the environmentalist type. You'll find many mangrove observation spots, fauna, and amazing landscapes which are picture – perfect.

Most expats and tourists love to do different recreational activities like sport – fishing, trekking or nature walks, surfing and other fun – filled adventures perfect for adrenaline junkies. If you are looking to settle in a place where you can thoroughly enjoy the beach and soaked in the Costa Rican culture, then why not go to the North Pacific side of the country? This region is usually where most tourists go to since it's also just a few hours away from the capital in San Jose. The tropical paradise here in the northern region is superb which is why it's also a place where most foreigners reside. You can also go to the famous Treasure Island where it is filled with fantastic pirate stories, and it also holds an important national heritage with many flora and fauna species.

When it comes to opportunities, expats can take advantage of the agricultural and cattle – raising industry, in the country. Costa Rica is one of the largest producers of tropical fruits and flowers as well as different plants, reforestation. The agricultural industry in the country is a booming activity that generates most of the jobs and business opportunities both for locals and foreigners. Most businesses in the country are also highly conscious of the ecology, and it can be seen in the way they operate the business. Many local agricultural companies work hand – in hand with different environmental organizations and recycling programs to ensure that there's little to no impact to the environment.

You can also find lots of basic services and utilities in the country such as gas stations, shopping centers as well as great accommodation facilities, and various local restaurants offering scrumptious Costa Rican and international cuisines.

If you're planning to move to the country with your kids, Costa Rica offers many different educational projects particularly in the creative industry. The country's priority as of this writing is to stimulate artistic activities. Most Costa Ricans are innately creative despite of their limited resources; the locals found a way to integrate what they're rich in – natural resources and creativity – and combined it with modern artful techniques.

Costa Rica is also filled with so much heritage and history. The buildings, monuments, and plantations can be traced back to the Afro – Caribbean culture. It is indeed a country bustling with amazing heritage preserved throughout the ages.

Even if the country has become one of the most popular tourist destination in Central America, Costa Rica still managed to maintain that laid – back way of living which made it popular in the first place. Most expats who come here are usually health conscious and/ or someone who deeply cares for the environments. You can find many community classes like various types of yoga class located in cities and beaches where most people relax throughout the week, you'll surely enjoy residing here.

Most foreigners instantly get attracted in living in the country because it gives off that bohemian vibe, culture, and real world spirit. Many expats come here to enjoy the crystal clear blue waters, untamed ocean, lustrous forests and jungles, wild fauna and flora, Caribbean food as well as the creative vibe from its people.

You'll definitely enjoy it here as most expats do because Costa Rica is a country bustling with different kinds of artists. Expats who usually settle here are from creative industries such as musicians, writers, filmmakers, photographers, and other creative professionals. There's also a sort of spiritual culture that Costa Rican embodies, and you can do other recreational activities like yoga, wellness programs, environmental activities, film and music fests and various adventures. The country is truly charming and you're days as an expat will surely be filled with many treasured moments and joy that will last forever. Simply, Costa Rica – Pura Vida!

Chapter One: An Overview of Costa Rica

What separates Costa Rica from other countries in the Caribbean is its striking combination of the familiar and the unknown. This is precisely the reason why the country attracts tourists and expats from all over the world. It has a certain character, and a level of sophistication which is sort of coming from its basic and unpretentious warmth from its environmental vibe as well as its people. If you're a foreigner looking for a place where you can live a much more comfortable and peaceful life without the stress of living in the hustles and bustles of city centers, and where you can thoroughly enjoy the outdoors and mingle with creative and friendly people, then there's no better place than Costa Rica.

It is a country that's located in the heart of an ecologically rich environment away from the chaos and the usual day to day living. It's a country worth exploring not just because it possess many great natural destinations but also because it is full of creative people from artists, writers, to musicians and performers who practices their craft and thrives despite of the limited technological resources found in modern day countries. If you're an expat who are into the creative industry or arts, then this is a great place to reside in because this is where you can truly commune and become one with nature which could bring about great ideas and inspiration that can translate into your work.

When it comes to economic conditions, Costa Rica's laid – back lifestyle wouldn't cost you an arm and a leg compared to other countries like the United States or Great Britain or other European countries or developed economies, this is because the way of living is quite better and the expat laws is less stringent. This is also one of the reasons why

Costa Rica attracts many expats as it give off that laid – back and exciting lifestyle and peaceful living conditions.

You can enjoy the many spectacular types of scenery in the country including landscapes, beach destinations, waterfalls, forests, and various fauna species. What's great is that even though it has witnessed hordes of tourist from all over the world, and real estate has been flourishing recently, it is still unfazed and not totally exploited. The country managed to preserve its many beautiful rocky cliffs, natural reserves, wild forests, and isolated beaches.

Speaking of beaches, Costa Rica is also the top destinations when summer hits because it has some of the most amazing beaches that also draws many surfers. You can expect to do lots of outdoor activities like mountain climbing, walking in the forests, bonding with exotic wildlife, and also socializing with its vibrant people and culture. Expats also love the country because of its great climate, fantastic local cuisine, lush environment, and peaceful lifestyle. This chapter will cover the general information about everything Costa Rica. Read on!

Costa Rica in Focus

Officially known as the Republic of Costa Rica, the country has become one of the most popular tourist destinations since the 1980's mainly because of its well – established national parks and naturally preserved areas. The land area of Costa Rica covers around 23%. It is home to a variety of flora and fauna, and it estimated to contain around 5% of biodiversity in the whole planet. Expats, tourists, and locals alike can enjoy many water sources because it is surrounded by both the Pacific Ocean and the

Caribbean Sea. There are also lots of active volcanoes, and a thriving metropolis.

Costa Rica is also quite a peaceful country because it managed to stay away from the violence, and various political turmoil in which most countries in Central America face today. In the 1940's Costa Rica's government abolished the army permanently, and the country also managed to be the only Latin American country to be included in the list of oldest democratic countries in the world. This goes to show how peaceful and stable the country is as a nation and from a political standpoint.

Costa Rica is also one of the most consistent Latin American countries in the Human Development Index. This means that it is a great place where one can discover and thrive in terms of human development.

It is of no surprise that the country also ranks high in the Environmental Performance Index. It was also recognized as the greenest country in the world. But that's not all! Costa Rica was also awarded by the NEF or New Economics Foundation as one of the happiest countries in the world particularly in 2009 and 2012. However, most travelers thinks that Costa Rica is the most expensive country to go to in Central America because things like entrance fees to tourist destinations, every day commodities such as coffee and wine is quite expensive and sometimes costs more than in North America or Europe. Nevertheless, it's a great country filled with diverse cultures, tropical forests, blue beaches, environmentally rich mountains and forests as well as great climate that anyone can surely enjoy.

A Brief History of Costa Rica

Let's look back at what went down in history and take note of some of the most significant events that took place which made the country what it is today, so that you can appreciate the Costa Rican culture even more and perhaps take part in its amazing future:

- 1502: Christopher Columbus arrived in the shores of the country and called it Costa Rica (Rich Coast).
- 1522: Gil Davila led an expedition to the country and converted Indians to Christianity.

- 1524: Spanish settlements were established which was led by Francisco Cordova.
- 1540's: Costa Rica becomes a part of vice – royalty of Spain.
- 1561: The first Spanish colony was established led by Juan Cavallon.
- 1821: The whole Central America gained independence from the Spaniards; dispute over Costa Rica joining a confederation of Central American states.
- 1823: Costa Rica becomes a part of the United Province of Central America together with Guatemala, Honduras, Nicaragua, and El Salvador
- 1838: Costa Rica achieved its independence.
- 1855: America, William Walker attempted to take over Costa Rica.
- 1849 – 1859: Juan Mora of Costa Rica led a resistance against William Walker.
- 1874: Banana cultivation in Costa Rica began
- 1919: US Marines invaded Costa Rica
- 1940: US Navy bought 2/3 of the Vieques island from $1.4 million

- 1940 – 1944: President Rafael Guradia recognized worker's right and wages and also introduced liberal reforms.
- 1949: New constitution was in effect: women including those of African descent were given the right to vote; army was abolished and replaced with civil guard. National banks were also introduced.
- 1978: Costa Rica experiences economic decline
- 2000: Costa Rica and Nicaragua finally settled the border dispute which was located in the San Juan River.
- 2007: CAFTA or Central American Free Trade Agreement was somewhat passed; Costa Rica also elected a non – permanent member of United Nations Security Council.
- 2009: Costa Rica re – established ties with Cuba after forty eight years.
- 2010: Costa Rica elected its first woman president named Laura Chinchilla.

Cities and Provinces in Costa Rica

This section will show you the provinces in Costa Rica, the capital within each province, and the estimated population in each city. You can also check out the population of major urban areas in the country in the next table. This will help you in deciding later on where you would want to reside.

Province	Abbreviation	Capital	Estimated Population (as of 2017)
Costa Rica	CRI	San Jose	4.9 Million
Alajuela	ALA	Alajuela	989,000
Cartago	CAR	Cartago	530,000
Guanacaste	GUA	Liberia	377,000
Heredia	HER	Heredia	505,000
Limón	LIM	Limón	444,000

Major Urban Areas

Provinces/ Cities	Abbreviation	Estimated Population (as of 2017)
San Jose	SJO	1.4 Million
Heredia	HER	356,000
Cartago	CAR	227,000
Alajuela	ALA	190,000

Puntarenas	PUN	83,000
San Isidro de El General	SJO	66,000
Limón	LIM	65,000
Liberia	GUA	56,000
San Rafael de Alajuela	ALA	55,000

Geography and Climate

Costa Rica borders Nicaragua to the north and Panama to the south. It comprises of around 51,000 square kilometers of land area, and around 590 square kilometers of territorial waters. The highest point and also the 5th highest peak in all of Central America are called Cerro Chirripo which stands at about 12,500 feet. The highest volcano stands at about 11,250 feet and it is called Irazu Volcano. The largest lake in the country is called Lake Arenal.

The country is composed of many islands including the Cocos Island and Calero Island (largest island in Costa Rica). Most of the country's national territory (around 25%) is protected by an organization called SINAC or the National System of Conservation Areas.

When it comes to the climate and weather, Costa Rica is famous for its tropical sunshine. It also experiences a temperate tropical climate due to cool wind breezes over the mountains. And since it is near the equator, the country only has 2 seasons: the dry season and rainy season. The dry season starts in December and usually ends around April, while the rainy season is from May to November.

The average temperature in Costa Rica is between 70 to 80 degrees. Even if it's quite close to the equatorial sun, its land orientation keeps the average temperatures down in almost all parts of the country. The elevation also somewhat affects the rainy microclimates in other regions.

Dry and Wet Season

The dry season starts around December and lasts until April. You can expect sunny and humid days with cool trade winds. When trade winds hit the northwest of Costa Rica, you can expect a very hot climate. It usually starts around March to April.

The cooler dry season starts around November to January since trade winds flow through the mountain around this time. The dry season also brings temperature fluctuations and can vary from 14 to 18 degrees in its days and nights.

The rainy season starts in the month of May until the first few weeks of November. You can expect a warm mornings and mild to heavy showers in the afternoon around July to August. Heavy downpours usually occur from September to October. There could be threats of flooding if you're residing near the riverside especially if there are typhoons.

Best Time to Visit Costa Rica

If you plan to reside in the country, it's wise to take a short visit just to check its climate and weather particularly in areas where you and your family are planning to live in. You can also see if the area around your neighborhood is safe if ever typhoons occur.

The best time to go here is of course during the dry season. Most budget travelers actually prefer going to the country during the rainy season because during this time hotel rates are much lower or at a discounted price. You might also get to see lesser crowds, and inexpensive lodging especially from August to October as there'll usually be less tourists around this time.

Language

Spanish is the official language of Costa Rica. You can actually learn to speak in Spanish quite easily here because their dialect is easier to understand especially if you're just starting to get a grasp of the language. The good news for foreign expats is that there are many schools and language centers that can help you learn the language. Usually, they offer group classes that last around 4 hours per day from Mondays to Fridays. Most schools also offer classes for families, and you may also choose other alternatives like student residence so that you can avail discounts.

When choosing a school where you can learn the Spanish language – Costa Rican way is to decide the best location where you can practice it. You don't want to go to schools located near the beaches as it may not give you a chance to practice the language since most tourists don't speak Spanish. However, some expats like to study near the beaches because they also go to other classes like surfing class or photography class. Obviously, if you really want to become fluent in the language, it's best if you live among the locals or try to reach out to them as much as you can and learn how to socialize.

Most expats reside in the capital in San Jose. There are not a lot of tourists in the city, but there are also lots of Spanish schools you and your family can attend in, the best part is that you can get immersed in the language since the setting and the people are mostly locals. This will prevent you from switching to your native language, and make you more comfortable in speaking like a true Costa Rican.

Social and Cultural Norms and Etiquettes

As part of your preparation in relocating to Costa Rica you need to be familiar with their customs and general etiquette. Learning and understanding the Costa Rican way of life will certainly help you in blending in and be able to adjust pretty easily. You can easily adapt their way of life by applying what you'll learn in this section. You can also practice it through mingling with the Costa Ricans, making new friends, and taking the various opportunities in your day to day living for you to learn their customs. Costa Ricans will surely forgive you for any cultural mistakes so if ever you do commit one, just laugh it off and keep getting better.

Greeting Etiquettes

As with most countries in Central America and South America, it's very common to say hello and goodbye to acquaintances with a light kiss on the cheek. Sometimes you can also "air kiss" or just make a kissing sound while lightly touching one's cheek. This is only done if you're a woman, and you're kissing either another women or men. Men usually greet other men with a hug or a handshake. Formal meetings usually start with a handshake for both genders.

Timeliness

Since the country is famous for its laid – back lifestyle, you can expect its people to be quite the laid – back type as well. Most of the locals observe what is known as the "tico" time or "la hora tica." This only means that Costa Ricans usually arrive late to any form of gathering. If you set up at meeting, say at 10 AM, you can expect them to arrive 30 minutes later or sometimes even a little later. This has been the people's way of living which is why it's not viewed as rude or a sign of being tardy. It's just the way they are, so better adjust your expectations.

The only time perhaps that the locals arrive on time is if they're going the doctor's appointment, the airport, or the movies as they'll need time to fall in line. It's also wise to clarify what time or date you're going to meet instead of vague responses.

Non – Confrontational People

Costa Ricans almost always want to avoid confrontation or accusations, and if ever they do, they do it in a very courteous and polite way so as not to offend the feelings of others. In short, they're not the straightforward type, and they won't also appreciate straightforwardness from other people especially from a foreigner. You won't see locals get angry in public even if they're sort of entitled to do so. This is because most of them are taught to practice peaceful ways of solving issues without the need of offending anyone at a young age.

They'll usually not say "no" to you even if they wanted to, so instead they'll say "maybe" or "I'll try." This is their way of not hurting other people's feelings, and again not meant to tell you a lie or mislead you.

Dress

Most locals dress up nicely especially during business situations and other important occasions or even simple family gatherings. Both genders dressed appropriately and formally though not in a conservative way like what how people dressed up in North America. You'll find that the formal attire to them usually involves splashy colors and a pair of jeans especially for women. You'll see that most women wear high heels and heavy makeup with sometimes revealing clothes, and not a suit or jacket except very formal affairs.

Taboos

Costa Rica is a very religious country. Just like most countries in Central America, they were occupied by the Spaniards and have since been converted as Catholics. They have high regard for religious values and observe it most of the time. Topics like abortion, marital sex, and gay marriage are usually avoided.

Unacceptable Behavior

Make sure to always say “please” and “thank you” and be as polite as possible. Never raise your voice especially in public, and try to resolve issues with ease and just be more patient if need be. Whenever you’re going to a person’s home, act politely and don’t put your feet up on the furniture. Greet everyone in the family as well.

You’ll find that small towns are much more conservative than the cities. Locations where there are always lots of tourists such as beaches and other tourist spots are more liberated. Nevertheless, just always be respectful and take the time to observe how people react or what their norms are in the area or neighborhood you’re going to relocate into so that you can properly manage your expectations and also adjust.

Gift Giving

Giving of gifts is usually practiced in the country especially during major occasions like the holidays, birthdays, Mother's day and Father's day. You can always bring it a bottle of wine or flowers if ever you'll be invited at a dinner party or celebrate in various events. Don't give out lilies as these are the flowers used in funerals.

Quick Facts

General Overview: Costa Rica is one of the most peaceful countries in Central America which is great for potential expats. It's also the only country without an army or military.

Location: It is near Nicaragua and Panama. Have ports in the Caribbean Sea and Pacific Ocean.

Country Capital: San José

Population: Men: 49.86%; Female: 50.14%

Density: 203 inhabitants per sq. mile

Government: Constitutional Government

Languages Spoken: Spanish and English

Longevity: Most Costa Ricans have an average life expectancy of 75 years.

Environmental Diversity: Due to its geographical location, Costa Rica is filled with fauna and flora. You'll find many mangrove observation spots, fauna, and amazing landscapes which are picture – perfect.

Habitat: lowland jungles to arid bare mountain peaks

Literacy Rate: 96. 2%

Public Health Services Coverage: 90% of the population

Health Expenditures: 27.8% of government total

Highest Point: Mount Chirripó

Chapter Two: Immigration

Everything related to residency in Costa Rica is handled by the Department of Immigration or the *Dirrecion General Migracion Y Extranjeria* which is located in the capital city of San Jose. The immigration law provides 3 main residency categories namely; permanent residency, temporary residency, and special categories which what you'll learn later on in the following pages. This chapter will cover everything you need to know about getting a temporary and permanent residency in Costa Rica for you and your family.

It will also include how you can live in the country by legally obtaining a residency status. If you check online, say from social media posts, blogs, and some websites there almost always lots of information, or should I say, misinformation about how foreigners can attain such status and get their residency visa which is why the goal of this chapter is to only give you nothing but facts directly coming from the Costa Rican Immigration policies and the immigration law.

This chapter will also provide you with a wealth of information about the different immigration categories - what are they, and what do you need to qualify; I'll also list the documents you'll need to apply for residency; the step by step application process and how it works or how you can file it; what happens once you've filed your application or what you can expect when waiting for the residency approval; and lastly, we'll give some tips on how you can claim your residency card and what you need to do once you or your family is approved.

Different Types of Immigration Programs in Costa Rica

Temporary Residency Immigration Program

Temporary residency is the most common initial classification or program that most expats or foreigners apply for in Costa Rica. There are different categories under the temporary residency program which we will lay out here, so just read it and see where you/ your family fits in. The 3 categories in availing a temporary residency visa are the following:

- Pensionado (Retiree)
- Rentista (Income Recipient)
- Investor (Inversionista)

Pensionado Residency (Retiree)

This means residency based on pension. This category perfectly fits expatriates who are already retirees and are looking to relocate in Costa Rica. Obviously, for you to qualify, you'll need pension – a lifetime pension. The minimum pension required is US$1,000 per month, and that includes your spouse and dependents (if any) in your application. Without having reached the minimum of a thousand dollars per month, you won't be able to acquire this type of visa. Examples of pensions include the following:

- Social Security
- Government Pension
- Disability Pension
- Private Pension

Acquiring any of the pensions mentioned above will qualify you to apply for temporary residency under the Pensionado program.

Rentista Residency (Income Based Residency)

The Rentista Residency program or category is available for foreign expats who don't have a pension. This is usually where most expats fall into. It will require you to prove that you have a monthly income of US$2,500. This amount will also include your spouse and any of your children under the age of 25 years old as they will serve as your dependents.

The easiest way to prove your income is to get a letter from your bank or financial institution, whether you're bank is in North America, Europe or Asia or even in Costa Rica; you'll need to acquire an official letter from them stating that you will receive US$2,500 per month for the next 2 years. The keywords that will help you are "permanent" and "stable." The reason for this is because that's what the law states.

Investor Residency (Income Based Residency)

As the name implies, it will require you to make an investment. The minimum investment is US$200,000. Once approved, it will include your spouse and any of your children under the age of 25 years old as they will serve as your dependents. This is more suitable if you're planning to move to Costa Rica for business purposes or if you're an entrepreneur/ investor in your own country as you'll need to prove that you have a capital.

You might be wondering what you need to invest in to qualify in this category. According to the law, you can invest the required amount in real estate or real property, purchasing shares of company or stocks, negotiable instruments, productive projects or projects that the country deems of national interest. The most important thing in this newly updated law is that, it now allows potential expats or foreigners to invest in real estate. This means you can qualify for temporary residency under this category by simply acquiring or purchasing a house, condominium, farms or perhaps vacation properties which is great because it's like hitting 2 birds with one stone. You can get approved as long as you have the capital, and also buy a house using that same capital.

What are the benefits of acquiring residency?

Most people ask this question; does it give me discounts or are there any sorts of task exemptions or are there any sorts of incentives like waving your import duties etc. Unfortunately, Costa Rica or having a temporary resident status doesn't give any of the things aforementioned or financial benefits other than acquiring a legal status to remain in the country.

The Application Process

Your application will need to be written in Spanish but for the purposes of this guide book, we'll break down what your application paper needs to contain in English. These are the information you'll need to provide before filing it in the Department of Immigration:

- Name of applicants
- Nationality
- Passport Number
- Date of Birth
- Occupation
- Name of Parents
- Entry Date to Costa Rica
- Income information
- Local Address
- Supporting Documents
- Where to receive notices
- Signature Date and Authentication (by a known republic)

Supporting Documents

This section will discuss the supporting documents that must accompany your residency application. This can also apply when applying for permanent residency visa.

Birth Certificate: must be acquired from the country you were born

Police Clearance Certificate: must be issued by the police authority in the country/ place you're currently residing

Marriage Certificate: for those applying with their spouses

Proof of Income Source: just like what was previously discussed. If you're applying for a Pensionado, then you need to show proof of a lifetime pension; if you're applying for Rentista, you need to acquire an income letter from your bank; if you're applying as an Investor provide documentation or proof of the investments you made such as property valuation/ land titles, certificate ownership, shareholder certification, C.P.A. certification and other additional documents depending on the type of investment you made.

Copy of Your Passport: you need to photocopy even the blank pages

Registration with your local Embassy: you can contact your local embassy to find out what the procedures are for registration.

Photographs: you must have at least 6 photographs for the entire process.

Power of Attorney: If you're being represented by a legal representative in Costa Rica, then you'll need Power of Attorney.

Hoja de Filiacion: This is a personal background form or paper. It is usually attached to the application/ documents for filing.

Authentication of Documents

The documents aforementioned need to go through an authentication process to be validated by the immigration officers of Costa Rica. If the country that issued the documents is a member of The Hague treaty then the document can be Apostille (a validation stamps ensuring public documents are recognized in foreign countries – countries that signed The Hague Convention Treaty). Both the U.S. and the European Union are members of this treaty which is why it will most likely follow this authentication procedure.

If your country is not a member of The Hague Convention Treaty then you have to follow the regular legalization process; after submitting your important documents, it will then go through the Government Certifying Authority, then the Foreign Relations Office, then verified by the Costa Rica Embassy or Consulate before being submitted to the Costa Rica Ministry of Foreign Relations. This is the steps included in the legalization process.

It's very important to translate all your documents to Spanish. You can use Official Translators provided by the Costa Rica Ministry of Foreign Relations website. You can search your language, and just hire a translator for you.

Filing the Application

Once your documents are all ready, you can now file it in the immigration office and pay the fee. You can also hire somebody to do the process for you so that you can save lots of time and headaches.

The application fee in Costa Rica will cost you US$50. You also have to pay Colones ₡125 plus 2.50 per page of the application (government filing fee). You might also pay US$200 if you wish to change your status. Once you've filed it, you'll be issued a receipt indicating you've filed an application and you'll also get to see your application file number.

Approval of Application

The approval process waiting time will depend on the file and how many applications are pending at the immigration office at the time. You can expect to wait around 7 to 15 months. Average waiting time is 12 months or 1 year. And once your application is approved, it is done so by the way of Resolucion by the Department of

Immigration. It is the final approval granting your or your family a residency status. Once you have this, the last step is to ask for an appointment at the immigration so that you can set the date of when you can pick – up your residency card.

Final Appointment for Residency Card

On the date of your final appointment to pick up your residency card (temporary or permanent). You need to ensure that you have a receipt of payment to Banco de Costa Rica for guaranty bond (around US$300); you need another receipt of payment to Banco de Costa Rica to cover the immigration use fee and residency card itself (around US$123). You'll also need your passport, and the proof of registration and payment to the "Caja" or the Costa Rica Health Care System. It's mandatory to pay through their health care system. And voila you're done!

General FAQs for Permanent Resident Visa

What is a Permanent Residency Visa?

Permanent residency visa is usually available for foreign expats who have an immediate family living in Costa Rica or is in a relationship with a Costa Rican citizen. This is also applicable for foreigners who already have held a temporary residency visa or status for around 3 years already.

What if I have immediate relatives in Costa Rica?

There is a program suited for those foreigners who have immediate relatives in Costa Rica that are already a permanent resident or a citizen. Usually it is applicable for those who are related in the first degree.

The law recognizes the following foreigners to qualify in this category:

- Parents of Costa Rican citizens
- The Minor Children of a Costa Rican citizen
- Children of a Costa Rican citizen that has a disability regardless of age

- Minors who are siblings of a Costa Rican citizen or siblings that have a disability regardless age.

What I married a Costa Rican?

Under the immigration law, the spouse should first apply as a temporary resident as aforementioned. The spouse of the Costa Rican citizen is usually given a temporary residency status for about a year and it can also be renewable for another year as long as the immigration authorities verified the authenticity of the marriage. After 3 years of holding a temporary visa, the spouse may now apply for the permanent residency visa status. Once you've finished 3 years, you are also eligible to file/ submit a petition for a change of status. The Department of Immigration will review it and it's up to them if you will be granted a resolution or not.

I intend to work in Costa Rica; can I apply for a permanent residency status?

Foreigners who intend to work in the country should have a temporary resident status before being able to apply for a permanent residency. Follow the procedures mentioned above.

What are the requirements and application process?

The process and requirements for permanent residency is very similar to that of the temporary residency application with a few additional requirements depending on your situation. The fees may also vary and the processing time especially if you are married or have relatives that is already a citizen or has a permanent residency status

Chapter Three: Expat Districts and Cost of Living in Costa Rica

Most expats wanting to relocate in Costa Rica usually pass up living in the capital of San Jose. Even if it's a cultural center and a place where all the "action" is, most foreigners prefer residing in areas that's actually away from the hustle and bustle of the city, since this is a country famous for its natural landscapes, sceneries, wildlife, and tranquil lifestyle which is the main reason why most expats relocate here.

Fortunately, even if you don't decide to live in the capital, everything is still within reach since most cities and small towns host many infrastructures, various facilities, establishments, important institutions, accommodation, restaurants, and above all tourism hotspots. Travelling to other towns or cities is quite accessible thanks to their transportation systems.

When it comes to choosing where to reside, it's best that you first consider your main purpose on why you want to move to Costa Rica in the first place. Is it for work? Is it because you are already retired? Do you have kids? Do you love trying out new things and going to various recreational adventures? Or do you just want to be immersed in the Costa Rican culture? Such things will help you consider the best region or place where you or your family will settle once you get here. It's also best if you ask people for recommendations or even fellow expats who are already living in Costa Rica just so you can have an idea of the kind of lifestyle in a particular place. You can also check out different expat forums online so that you can have an idea if a certain area that you are eyeing best suits your needs and that of your family.

In this chapter, you will be given an overview of each of the top districts in Costa Rica where expatriates commonly live. We'll give you a list of quick info that you need to know about each place we suggested here and what you can expect when it comes to the cost of living in Costa Rica. This can all help you make an informed decision so that you can decide accordingly based on your preferences.

San Jose, Costa Rica: The Capital

There are many advantages if you reside in the capital. Even if San Jose is just a small city based on world capital standards, it still has the widest range of options when it comes to housing – which is one of the first things you need to consider before relocating. Each of the areas within the capital can offer you different housing options such as subdivisions/ villages, condominium complexes, and suburbs that offer different options from single – family residences, student dorms, to affordable apartments perfect for renting or purchasing.

Below is a quick overview of what's it like to stay in any of the towns or "barrios" within San Jose:

- **Barrio Escalante:** If you're a history buff or someone who appreciates the historical facet of the country, then this is the place for you. Barrio Escalante is the historic section in San Jose. Aside from that, there are also lots of local and international restaurants, marvelous parks, museums, and also cultural centers. If you're the kind of person who likes to get around on foot or loves urban areas, this is one of those towns. The only downside is that Barrio Escalante is known as the central of sex tourism in the country; expect lots of prostitutes around the area. Definitely not for expats with kids.

- **Belen:** The town of Belen is regarded as one of the best – managed municipalities in the country. It's located in the western suburb of the capital and it's very close to many important establishments like the airport, multinational companies. It's also bordered by 2 major high ways making transportation quite accessible. Most expats with families and those who are working usually lives here because the neighborhoods are safe, and you can find lots of option when buying single – family homes.

- **Escazu or Santa Ana:** This is also located in the western suburbs of the capital. This is the place that attracts mostly the wealthy locals and expats. The real estate in this town is filled with chic apartments, high – rising condominiums, and it's also home to the highest – priced real estate in the country. There are also lots of high – end restaurants, shopping malls, and transportation is also very accessible.

- **Heredia:** This is a place in San Jose where you can find lots of residential communities ranging from local and expat families to foreign students. It is home to many universities in Costa Rica as well. The place also attracts many tourists because of the amazing views of the city, and various development activities. The only downside is that because of all these activities and foot traffic, the place is not commuter friendly.

- **Los Yoses:** This is where you can find many foreign embassies and government offices as well as private companies. It also has several quiet residential neighborhoods which is perfect for those who want to live in quite a tranquil way but not too far from the city – center. All necessities are very convenient and is usually walking distance; transportation is also accessible as there are many bus lines to and from this town.

- **La Sabana:** If you're a young professional, then this is the right place for you. You can find many people here who are in their 20's and 30's. It's also quite close to the city – center. Many bars and restaurants abound the area, and it also has great neighborhoods.

- **San Pedro:** This is another place where most foreign students reside in since the country's main universities are located here namely; Universidad de Costa Rica, and Universidad Latina. If you're looking for an affordable place while studying here, you can find lots of apartments and dormitories that are usually affordable. You can even choose to share the rent with 3 to 4 people as there are lots of bedroom type houses in the area. There are lots of cheap places where you can eat and shop, and most necessities are also walking distance.

Puerto Jimenez

Quick Facts:

- **Area:** Osa Peninsula
- **Avg. Temperature:** 27° C
- **Landscape:** Mostly beaches and tropical rainforests
- **Activities:** Wildlife tours, kayak riding, fishing, outdoor adventures
- **Attractions:** Golfo Dulce, Corcovado National Park, Osa, Wildlife Sanctuary, Playa Puntarenitas, Cabo Matapalo
- **Nearby Airports:** Juan Santa Maria Int'l Airport, Puerto Jimenez Airstrip
- **Public Transportation:** Frequent bus service to and from the area of Matapalo and from San Jose
- **Stores:** There are lots of small markets nearby, various food stands, local shops, and restaurants
- **ATMs:** Yes
- **Banks:** No
- **Schools:** No
- **Gas Stations:** Yes

- **Wi – Fi/ Mobile Coverage:** Most areas have a coverage though signal may vary. Has a reliable connection
- **Medical Facilities:** Has small clinics but the nearest hospital is a boat ride away

Puerto Jimenez is the largest town located in the Osa Peninsula. You can expect to have a relax way of life here as with most places in Costa Rica. The area is filled with many stunning beaches which are also best for expats who are into swimming and different watersports. The waters here are also tranquil, and it is a great place to experience scuba diving and snorkeling activities. You can also see lots of sports fishing action here since it is also home to many different fish species like the roosterfish, amberjack, and African Pompano which are really hard to catch and can test the skills even for experienced fishermen. If you're not into the water scene, don't worry because you can go on to wildlife tours since there is also lots of tropical paradise in the area that's also very accessible from the town center.

Some of the activities most tourists and expats do include sightseeing, feeding tours, excursions, mangrove kayaking, visiting botanical gardens, and interacting with many wildlife species as well as various fauna and floras.

Puerto Jimenez has a humid tropical climate, and if you're planning to visit the place, the best time to go is from November to April. The town is also known for its eco – lodges, which mean that most hotels here observe environmental friendly accommodations combined with modern luxuries with authentic Costa Rican tropical experience. If you decide to reside here, you'll pretty much be nestled in forests. You can find lots of boarding houses downtown as well as many international and local cuisines.

The restaurants here are superb because you'll get to taste the best of Costa Rican cuisine combined with Asian, South American and European influences. And since Puerto Jimenez is a coastal town, seafood is the main staple of food here. The nightlife here is also fantastic; you can find many great bars and places at night that offers local experience and cuisines.

Golfito

Quick Facts:

- **Best for:** Families, solo travelers, adventure seekers, nature lovers
- **Public Transportation:** very accessible; has many public buses, and taxi boats are also available
- **Stores:** There are lots of groceries, stores, shops and boutiques
- **ATMs:** Yes and there are also several banks
- **Gas Stations:** Yes
- **Wi – Fi/ Mobile Coverage:** Has a reliable connection; most restaurants and coffee shops have coverage
- **Medical Facilities:** Has public hospitals; private clinics and also a couple of pharmacies
- **Attractions:** Piedras Blancas National Park, Playa Zacundo, Playa Payones, Playa Cabo Matapalo
- **Activities:** Trekking, surfing, scuba diving, kayaking, snorkeling, swimming, bird watching, sports fishing, mountain biking, horse riding, whale/ dolphin watching

Golfito is another tourist spot where some expats also choose to reside in. It's located in the Southern region of Costa Rica near Panama and on the eastern side of Golfo Dulce. The port is become quite prosperous especially around the 20th century because of the United Banana Company up until 1985. Now it has regained its popularity because it became a tourist spot and also became the Golfito Reserve also known *Refugio Nacional de Vida Silvestre*. There are also lots of national parks around and also offers the most interesting boat trips in all of Costa Rica.

One of the most treasured places here is the Corcovado National Park which is also extended up to Puerto Jimenez. It is recognized by National Geographic as being the best place on earth that is preserve in terms of biodiversity. This is also a place that attracts lots of surfers. Some expats live up in the high hills called San Vito. It is a small village founded by Italians sometime around the 50's. If you're someone who truly wanted to experience living a tranquil lifestyle or you're someone looking for an adventure, you can check it out. The climate in this area is also quite humid.

You can also find lots of botanical gardens and parks like the Wilson Botanical Garden where you can find around 700 species of palms, as well as the International Park La Amistad where you can find lots of indigenous tribes like the Bribri, Naso, Cabecar, Ngobe and also other similar Latin ethnic groups.

Playa Zancudo is the most visited beach here in Golfito. You can take a bus or a boat trip to get here. It is a long beach with lots of bars, restaurants, and shops around as well as small cabins. It's also a great place for surfing and sport fishing.

You can find lots of hotels here that are beautifully located in tropical setting. The place also offers many great international restaurants like Pizzeria Alery, Mary Luna, Rio de Jainero, and Le Coquillage. This place is mostly for expats looking for an adventure or those who are solo travellers.

Cartago

- **Area:** Central Valley & Highlands
- **Avg. Temperature:** 25° C
- **Landscape:** Valleys; elevated landscapes
- **Activities:** white water rafting, trekking, leisure tours in National parks and botanical gardens, hiking
- **Attractions:** Irazu Volcano, Our Lady of the Angels Basilica, Reventazon River, Lankester Botanical Gardens, Savegre Reserve, Chirripo National Park
- **Nearby Airports:** Tobias Bolanos International Airport
- **Public Transportation:** Regular buses from and to San Jose; has limited shuttle buses to nearby attractions
- **Stores:** There are lots of small markets nearby, various food stands, local shops, and restaurants
- **ATMs:** Yes
- **Banks:** Yes
- **Schools:** Yes
- **Gas Stations:** Yes

- **Wi – Fi/ Mobile Coverage:** Most areas have a coverage though signal may vary. Has a reliable connection
- **Medical Facilities:** Max Peralta Jimenez Hospital, Cartago

Cartago was actually Costa Rica's first capital until 1823. It's also where early Spaniards established settlements way back in the 16th century. It is the country's largest and oldest city. Unfortunately, due to the frequent eruption of the Irazu Volcano which is the most active in Costa Rica until today, most Spanish building built centuries ago were destroyed but despite of that it is still one of the country's most historic city, and it's still a very cultural place until today.

Famous buildings include Our Lady of the Angels Basilica locally known as Basilica de Nuestra Senora de los Angeles. Most devotees go here to see the famous sculpture of La Negrita or the Black Madonna. Aside from churches, there are also other historical architectures in this town.

You can find many tourists here especially Catholic pilgrims because every year they gather for different religious celebrations. Cartago is a place where you can start getting immerse in the Costa Rican culture and heritage aside from its stunning tropical surroundings.

If you're into nature, then visiting the Lankester Botanical Garden is a must. It is home to various types of exotic plants and that can only be found in Costa Rica and all of Central America. You can find lots of orchid collections, and also perfect for picture taking because of its spectacular colors. Similar to Puerto Jimenez, the best time to go is from November to April since it also has that quite humid climate.

There are lots of different accommodations that you and your family can avail during your trip to the countryside. You can also enjoy lots of great restaurants and nightlife. Cartago is famous for its home – cooked meals and haute cuisines. There are also lots of family – owned bakeries that specializes pastries and desserts.

Puntarenas

- **Area:** Central Pacific
- **Avg. Temperature:** 33° C
- **Landscape:** Beach and port
- **Activities:** surfing, scuba diving, boat cruises, windsurfing, canopy tours
- **Attractions:** Puntarenas Marine Park, Museo Historico Marino (Marine History Museum), La Casa de la Cultura Art Gallery, Tortuga Island, Carara National Park, Penas Biancas National Park
- **Nearby Airports:** Florencia Airport
- **Public Transportation:** regular buses to Jaco, intercity bus service, ferry ride to Nicoya Peninsula
- **Stores:** There are lots of outdoor markets nearby, various food stands, local shops, and souvenir vendors
- **ATMs:** Yes
- **Gas Stations:** Yes
- **Wi – Fi/ Mobile Coverage:** Most areas have a coverage though signal may vary. Has a reliable connection

- **Medical Facilities:** Costa Rica Social Security System Hospital

Puntarenas is the biggest port in Costa Rica making it a key destination for large cruise ships. It's also the gateway to the Nicoya Peninsula. Puntarenas, meaning sandy point, is actually both a city and province in the country. It is built on sandy spit of land near the Gulf of Nicoya surrounded in the 3 sides of water. The city is also known as El Puerto in Costa Rica. It is Costa Rica's principal sea port and was originally the transit center for coffee crop. Today many expats and foreign tourists go here to enjoy the beach since it is one of the closest in the capital of San Jose. If you reside here, pristine beaches are just a few walks away.

Both locals and foreigners alike love to come here because there are many annual celebrations, festivities, parades, and live events including concerts, sports competitions, and firework displays. There's so much to see in Puntarenas if you and your family decide to live here. You can also visit Tortuga Island, and see others exotic marine creatures.

Puntarenas have many housing options for different kinds of expats whether you have a family or a solo – traveller. You can find lots of family – owned eateries and top quality seafood cuisines.

Cost of Living in Costa Rica

Most foreign expats relocate in Costa Rica because the cost of living is still relatively cheaper but while most things are inexpensive, luxuries done in the North American way, can still add up. This section will give you an overview of how much it will cost you on average to live in any city or province in Costa Rica. This will give you an idea so you can gauge your budget and adjust your lifestyle accordingly.

Average Cost per Month

If you're the kind of person who lives a simple lifestyle, and only cares for your daily duties, you can budget around US$1,500 more or less per month. This will enable you to ride buses to and from different cities, take taxis occasionally, and also eat in nice restaurants every month. Other expats especially the retirees choose to live a more luxurious lifestyle. If you are like that, you may need to budget US$3,000 or more every month, this amount can cover your daily consumption, can afford you to hire housekeepers, lets you enjoy many trips and vacations, and also lets you sustain a living in high – end villages.

Housing Costs

Renting a place in most rural and urban areas can cost anywhere between US$300 and $600. With this amount you can most likely rent a small house or a well – furnished apartment. You can also expect to have other amenities included like laundry, and bathrooms with showers. If you purchase a 3 bedroom house near the capital or directly in San Jose, you can expect to pay rent of about $1,500 per month but of course it comes with the most luxurious amenities like Jacuzzi bathtubs and a home with granite tiles.

Food and Dining

Obviously, the cost will depend on where you'll eat and how much you'll eat. On average though, most restaurants with a complete meal like a main course, salad and red wine can cost around $15 to $20 per pax. If you eat at some sort of small eateries around the area where local foods are served, a meal and a fresh drink will only cost you $2 to $4. If you're going to cook for your family, you can easily get ingredients from local grocery stores or farmer's market and can cost you around $20 to $40; this is complete with meat, veggies, fruits and other goodies. Premium or imported goods will most likely cost more, and if you also buy from high – end grocery chain, expect to pay a minimum of $200 or more for a 1 week worth of groceries.

Goods, Services and Entertainment

In Costa Rica, services and labor is very cheap. You can hire a housekeeper and it will only cost you US$2 per hour. The gas however is quite expensive more than the cost in United States; you'll most likely pay about $1 to $2 more per gallon.

When it comes to entertainment, going to museums and cultural establishments tickets usually cost $5 per person. Wildlife adventures and entrance fees to tourist spots will likely cost more depending on the kind of activity you and your family will do.

Health Care

Medical care in the country is also quite inexpensive. Most locals are covered by either their private insurance or the government system under the Costa Rican Social Security. Medical insurances costs around US$60 to $150 per month

Estimated Breakdown of Cost of Goodies

Food	Average Cost (Costa Rican Colon)
Lunch with drinks in Restaurants	₡4,000
Fast Food Combo Meal	₡3,944
1 litter of milk	₡740
12 eggs	₡1,535
1 kilogram of tomatoes	₡1,260
1 kilogram of potatoes	₡1,046
1 bottle of red wine	₡6,000
Bread (good for 1 day)	₡1,024

Clothes	Average Cost (Costa Rican Colon)
1 pair of jeans (branded)	₡37,016

1 dress/ top dress (branded)	₡27,024
1 pair of rubber shoes (branded)	₡57,140

Transportation/ Commute	**Average Cost (Costa Rican Colon)**
1 liter of gas	₡615
Ticket for public transportation (taxis, buses, trains for 1 month)	₡24,000
1 pair of leather shoes (branded)	₡53,770

Personal Care/ Utilities	**Average Cost (Costa Rican Colon)**
1 month worth of electricity, gas, heaters etc.	₡42,950
1 month of Internet connection	₡30,199

Fitness Club (per month)	₡30,092
Cinema (1 person)	₡3,500
Pre – school (private monthly for 1 child)	₡206,000
International Primary School (per year for 1 child)	₡4,026, 149.98
Apartment in City Center (1 bedroom)	₡297,700

Chapter Four: Housing and Estate Planning

After fixing all the legal papers and considering what place you'll reside in, the next step is to ensure that you will be well – accommodated in the town/ city you chose so that you can easily adjust living in Costa Rica. Doing your due diligence before relocating or even considering moving to Costa Rica is a must! Once you've done that and have determined your purpose as what was mentioned in previous chapters, it's now time to think about how you will be accommodated once you get here. There are lots of people who will tell you that renting before purchasing a house is wise, though it can be a great option, there's also some disadvantages in doing that.

This chapter will give you some ideas on how you or your family can decide whether buying a house or renting a place is the best option for you. We will also provide you with easy steps on the process of acquiring a property and also tips about how estate planning is done in Costa Rica.

Renting vs. Buying

Moving to any country for any reason - whether you're planning to retire, do business, study, or simply experience a new way of living – is a very big step. This is the reason why figuring out your purpose, lifestyle, budget, and needs or that of your family is important because this is where everything will be based especially when thinking about acquiring a house or renting a property.

When considering whether to buy or rent it's essential to ask how long you'll be staying in the country – are you a temporary expat or are you planning to become a permanent resident? What's your purpose? The next question is who are you with? Are you a solo traveller or will your family come along? If so how many are you? How much have you saved up or how much is your budget? And will it be enough to buy a house? Answering these questions will determine if it's a better option for you to rent for the meantime and then just save up afterwards if you decide to buy your own property or if you'll maximize your money more when you directly acquire a property or a house.

If you're the kind of person who have rented your whole life, then renting is something that you are comfortable and familiar with. If you're not yet sure if you'll be staying in Costa Rica for the next 5 to 10 years, then renting is best for you. The main advantage of renting is it will not force you to make any long – term commitments. This is a great option especially if you're not used to the South American or Central American culture. According to statistics, 40% of foreign expats who moved to Costa Rica returned to their home countries or decided to leave the country within a year just because of culture shock! If you're not someone who can adapt quickly, it's best that you rent for a few months and see how it will work out for you.

On the other hand, there are also many advantages to owning a home or property in Costa Rica. These are some of the pros when buying a house instead of renting out one:

- **A place where you can call your own:** If you're someone who have owned a house ever since, then obviously renting a home may make it quite difficult for you, even if you bring all your furniture. You won't get everything like you want it to be, you'll usually have to settle for less because the garden will not like how you dream it to be or the kitchen will look different, and you may not be able to renovate the house or change the painting of the walls since it's not yours. You will pretty much lack personal touches in your home if you rent which is one of the disadvantages because this can also help you in adjusting to your new environment.

- **You can ask for professional help and also get advice when you buy from a realtor:** In renting, *o*nce you've already closed a deal with your landlord, you're pretty much on your own. You'll have to figure everything out for yourself. Don't expect that the landlord will help you if ever you encounter any difficulties regarding the house – this is what most foreign expats have experienced. On the other hand, if you purchase a house from a professional real estate broker or agent, you will get yourself a responsible advisor that won't just help you in purchasing a house or selecting a property but also help you in navigating your way in the fine details of living in the country. In short, they have what salesman called the "after sale." This is very important and usually the reason why lots of expats who bought a home didn't look back.

- **Purchasing a house gives you something to come back to:** Most expats buy properties in Costa Rica and make it their vacation house. The downside to this though is that you won't have the motivation to stay longer or adapt the Costa Rican culture because it can give you an excuse to just leave. Nevertheless, it's still a good thing because you have something to come back to.

- **You won't have to deal with landlords.** I'm not generalizing that all landlords in Costa Rica is hard to deal with but according to most foreign expats who rented a place most of the time it's hard to communicate to their landlords and they are also difficult to come to terms especially if you need help in fixing or replacing stuff around the house.

- **Buying a house is the best option for the long – term.** The reason for this is because you will be able to maximize your money compared to renting a house say for a few years. There are lots of foreign expats who regretted not buying a house or property after years of renting because they realize that they could've maximized their money since the purchase prices would have been much better.

FAQs When Purchasing a House/ Property in Costa Rica

There are many expats who don't know where to begin when it comes to purchasing a real estate property in Costa Rica. This section will answer all of the things you need to know when it comes to owning a property, the process involves, and where you should purchase it.

Can a foreigner acquire a real estate in Costa Rica?

Any expats whether you're a resident or not has the same rights as a Costa Rican (except of course for voting) when it comes to owning properties and/or doing work/ business. Therefore, yes buying a property, a land and/or a house and lot is legal. The only exception to this is that a foreigner cannot 100% own a property in the Maritime Zone, and an INDER property which is the land given by the government to poor farmers.

Will I get a title for any property I'll buy?

Yes, most properties in the country have a title. As long as your property is within the 50 meter high tide line, it is protected and also public. However, if you purchase (49%) land that is within the Maritime Zone, you'll most likely not get a title, and such concessions should be verified by the municipality. It's best to consult a legal lawyer before purchasing properties located within the Maritime Zone.

It could also be possible that the land you want to acquire is in the possession of the locals who live there, the downside to this is that you'll only get a title after 10 years but this is subject to change.

Will I have title insurance?

Even though most locals never avail title insurance, it is available nevertheless, and can be done if that's what you prefer. You can get title insurance for any of the property you purchase by searching online for real estate companies in Costa Rica that offers this service.

Are there any restrictions when it comes to purchasing properties near protected areas?

Yes. Costa Rica has many protected areas to ensure that nature is preserved and conserved. This can be a problem if you wish to acquire a property that is near rivers or forests. Each city in Costa Rica has its own zoning plan which you should check when buying a land. This will show you if the land you like is within the agricultural or residential zone. There are also restrictions for each zone, and you can request for a copy in the appropriate office within the municipality. Consult a real estate agent or lawyer about this.

Where can I get a copy of the property title/ land title?

All titled lands and properties including those that are within the Maritime Zone are registered in the website of the National Registry. Almost all land titles and certifications as well as powers of attorney, and registered surveys have a soft copy and can be requested via their website at <http://www.rnpdigital.com/index.htm>

Do I need to hire a real estate lawyer?

Yes. This is highly recommended. Foreigners and even citizens should hire a real estate lawyer whenever they're purchasing a property. It's also much better if you hire someone who specializes in real estate/ notary public that's also bilingual so that you are properly represented. One of the jobs of your notary public is to record your land purchase in the National Registry through a protocol deed. When hiring a real estate lawyer in Costa Rica, ensure that they have a SUGEF approved escrow account so that money can be held in escrow without legal problems.

How do I start finding a property or a house?

You can start searching online for locations, type of houses, and estimated prices that matches your preference. You can also visit the country every now and then or at least months before you make the move so that you can survey the area of where you like to reside in. Most foreigners avail a retirement tour which you can book online as this will help you kick start your property search.

Do I need to hire a real estate agent? Where can I find one?

You can easily search online any real estate companies that can help you in the area or region you prefer. You need to ensure that if you're not going to get an agent from a company, you should check if the freelance real estate agent you'll hire is someone who's an expert in the area you chose so that you can ask help once you make the move and even after you relocated. It's also wise to just pick one agent so that you can get the best option and narrow down your decision.

How much is the real estate commissions?

Usually commissions start from 5% to 7%. If there's an exclusive listing agreement, then commissions can be at 8% or more depending on the agency/company you chose. This wouldn't be a problem on your part since the company or the seller of the land is the one responsible in giving commissions to their real estate agents. If ever you do hire a buyer's agent, they'll most likely split their commission with the listing agent unless the property is foreclosure.

How do I make an offer on the property?

It's important that you don't try and make any sort of verbal offers. It's wise that you consult with your agent so that he/she will be the one to write an offer and propose it to the seller. Once it is agreed upon, you can ask your real estate agent to discuss it with your lawyer to create a formal purchase – sale agreement. When both you and the seller signed the agreement, there'll be an automatic 10% of the sales price that'll go into escrow with your real estate lawyer.

What if I can't be there for the closing deal?

If this is the case then you can use the special power of attorney to your real estate agent or anyone you trust that will allow a person or company that you approved of to acquire the property on your behalf.

What about the escrow?

It's best that you wire the complete acquisition price as well as legal fees into your escrow way before the closing date because Costa Rican banks will need to comply with money laundering laws which if you don't do can hold the money for several days.

How do I register the title in my name or other legal entity?

When you acquire a property in Costa Rica, you can register it under your name. If ever you would like to share the title with your spouse, family member and/or business partners but you don't want to allow them to sell it without your consent, then you can share the title in equal parts as a "right" or "derecho" in Costa Rica. You can also acquire a property in a corporation similar to an LLC, in Costa Rica is known as Sociedad Responsabilidad Limitada (SRL). Consult your lawyer regarding this kind of transaction.

Is there a title transfer cost?

You can transfer the title of your property to another company, another name or from a company to your own name. There'll usually be a 5% to 6% cost for title transfers from the total of the sales prices. There'll also be other miscellaneous fees like legal stamps, transfer taxes, and other notary fees.

What about the yearly estate taxes?

After paying the real estate transfer taxes, you'll also need to pay the yearly property tax in the municipality where your land is located. It will cost approximately 0.25% at the closing. Once closed, the seller should bring a certification to the municipality state that the property taxes are paid properly and up to date. All the receipts should be complete. Ask your lawyer about how much annual property tax you will need to pay as it will vary depending on the location and type of home.

Is there are corporation tax if I purchase my property from a corporation?

In 2012, the government of Costa Rica created a corporation tax, however, it was declared unconstitutional in 2015. As of this writing, we don't know if the law has been approved the Costa Rican congress. Consult with your lawyer about this.

What if I purchase a condo?

When you buy a condo, the seller should have a letter of the condominium administration and show proof that the HOA fees are duly paid.

What about housing utilities?

Once your real estate lawyer registered the title in the National Registry, you can now have your own residency ID. By having this, you can now go to the water, power and phone company to change the services under your name. The ID will serve as your proof of residency and ownership of the property.

Is it okay to leave my property without any caretakers?

Definitely not, if you're going to abandon your land or house and you don't hire anyone to take care of it, some squatters might move in without you knowing it. So better leave it with someone you trust or hire a caretaker to do make sure that your property is well – maintained and safe from any possible trespassers.

Estate Planning

In Costa Rica, when a person dies without a valid Will, it will be considered as "intestate." Therefore the person's asset including properties will be ruled under the intestacy laws. The regulations of the said law can be found in the Civil Code of Costa Rica. It states that in cases of invalid

Wills or absence of a Will, the assets or properties of the deceased will be automatically transferred to its legitimate heirs or next of kin. This is the reason why preparing a last Will and Testament is very important especially if you have many estates/ assets as this will avoid any inconvenience to the ones you left behind. It will also allow you to determine how your estate will be managed and distributed among the heirs you will choose. It will also allow you to choose the rightful executor.

Definition of Legitimate Heirs under the Civil Code

1st Degree: Includes the spouse, children and parents of the deceased. However, they are still subject to the following:

- If the husband/ wife have requested or were granted a legal separation; thus he or she will not be able to inherit any estate or asset.

- If the spouse is separated but not legally, the husband/ wife will only inherit part of the estate of the deceased since being separated.

- If ever the property is classified as a community property, the spouse will inherit a portion of the estate that is owned by the deceased.

- The parents of the deceased son or daughter will only inherit the estate if it is (a) born out of wedlock, (b) was recognized with his or her mom's consent, (c) if the parent/s were supported by the deceased son/ daughter for at least 2 consecutive years.

- If the deceased has a partner but is unmarried, the surviving partner may only inherit a portion of the estate if they both had the legal capacity to marry, and if they have co – inhabited for at least 3 years.

2nd Degree: Grandparents and other legit descendants of the deceased.

3rd Degree: Siblings on the mother's side of the deceased (natural brothers and sisters)

4th Degree: Nephews of the deceased

5th Degree: Uncles of the deceased

6th Degree: The State (Board of Education of the district where the property of the deceased is located).

Types of Wills in Costa Rica

There are two types of wills; the Non – Cupative will or commonly known as Open Will and the Closed will, also known as Sealed Wills.

Open Will

- The Open Will has two possibilities; the Attested, and the Notarized. The most common form in Costa Rica is the Notarized Will.

Notarized Will

This is usually drafted by the public attorney's office, and also executed before three witnesses, and they will swear about the physical, moral, and mental capacity of the Testator.

Usually married couples opt to execute a so – called Mutual Will wherein they both appoint each other as the rightful heir to all the possessions they have in Costa Rica. In the event that both of them died, both their children will serve as the universal beneficiaries of the Will and Testament for their estates/ assets in Costa Rica.

For the Will to be effective, it should indicate the following:

- Exact place, time, date, month, and year in which it is executed
- Read by a Notary Public or Testator in the presence of three witnesses
- Duly signed by the Notary Public, witnesses, and Testator, and it should be simultaneously executed.

Close Will

- The Close Will may or may not be the Testator's own handwriting.
- The content of the Will is not disclosed to anyone except the Testator

- There are specific formalities that will be followed in order to make it valid.

Executing a Will in Costa Rica

- This is a form of alternative when it comes to estate planning.

- The Will in Costa Rica is mostly limited to disposing of the assets/ estates within the territory of Costa Rica only.

- Therefore, all the assets/ estates of the deceased in Costa Rica will be probated with the Will to avoid all the judgment recognition procedure

- Legal advice is highly recommended to avoid or resolve any inconsistencies with the other Wills granted in another country.

Chapter Five: Utilities and Communication Services in Costa Rica

In Costa Rica primary utilities like electricity, water, and gas are usually included in the residence or rental house. You'll just have to sign papers or go directly to the office of providers in the area so that you can properly set up an account. You'll need to fill up forms and provide your personal details, and other necessary documents like a residency ID or your residency visa since you are a foreigner. It's best that you inform your provider at least a week or two before you moved in your new home so that it'll be up and running. If you're renting, the utilities and connections are usually bundled, and it's also customary to keep the bill under the name of the owner of the property/ house. Make sure to clarify it with your landlord, and ask him or her about your payment options. This chapter will provide you with general information about how to set up the needed housing utilities. We'll also give you an overview of the different mobile and internet plans that are available in Costa Rica so that you can make a comparative review of each.

Housing Utilities

Assuming that you've already bought a property/ house in Costa Rica for your move or perhaps you've already sealed the deal with your landlord if you choose to rent, the next thing to think about is the housing utilities. If you plan on renting a house, it's wise to ask beforehand if housing utilities such as water connections, electricity, gas, and even cable/phone lines are already available or if it's already inclusive of your rent. Usually, if you rent or bought a fully furnished house such as a condo, utilities are already included as well as other amenities.

This section will guide you on what you need to know regarding housing utilities and the process if ever you need to install it yourself.

Some Reminders Regarding Housing Utilities for those who are Renting

- In Costa Rica, the electricity, water meters, and telephone lines usually carry the landlord's name and not the tenant. This rule may be included in your lease agreement. If otherwise, you'll most likely need to go directly to the power, water or telephone company to install the services under your name.

- It will be up to you, the tenant, to install other communication services such as internet, cable TV, mobile, and also the gas. If ever such services are already installed, then you don't need to disconnect it, you just have to change it under your name.

- As long as you pay your bills on time either to your landlord or under his/her name, you won't have any trouble.

Gas

Gas in Costa Rica is usually propane gas. It is called Gas Licuado or GLP. You can purchase propane gas in grocery stores. You'll initially have to buy your own gas tank and just have it refilled in retail stores. You might get to encounter barbecue gas tanks which usually have a different valve than propane gas tanks, if ever this is what you've purchased, ask the store if it's possible to refill it with.

Water Utilities

In Costa Rica, the water company is owned by the government, but it is also possible that your house or the house you're renting is serviced by a private corporation or a cooperative. Some residential homes are covered by ESPH especially in Heredia, Costa Rica. Make sure to ask your real estate agent/ seller about it before purchasing or renting a house.

Electricity

CNFL is an electric company that is also owned by the government, and this is the power company that is servicing mot cities in Costa Rica. There are also other private companies that offer power services like ICE, JASEC and ESPH for remote areas such as Cartago, Heredia, Consorcio Conelèctricas, Coopeguanacaste, Coopesantos, Coopealfaroruiz, and Coopelesca.

Phone Lines, Internet Services, Cable TV Providers

Since the emergence of the mobile industry, telephone lines are already becoming obsolete in Costa Rica (except for offices/ business establishments). Most residents have already gotten rid of their telephones and have already switched to using either cellphones or digital phones that is often bundled with the TV or internet packages.

Phone services and communication services are controlled and provided by the government through the ICE but there are also other private owned companies such as Kolbi, Claro, Movistar, Sky Satellite TV, and Tigo that offers phone services, mobile plans, internet and cable TV packages. Later we will give you an overview of the services each of these providers offer so that you can have an idea of what their rates are and the features of each.

How to Apply for Housing Utilities

This is applicable for those who bought their own house without any service installation yet, or for those whose previous owners have disconnected their utility connections. Before you get power, communications, and water connections under your name, you must be a legal resident of the country, and show proof like a residency ID or a temporary/ permanent resident visa. If ever you bought a property under a corporate/ business name, then you need to get the utilities under the corporate/ business name. You can ask assistance from your legal attorney and use the special power of attorney to get such utilities under your name/ business' name.

Legal Residents Registration

If you're already a resident, and you have already been issued a valid residency card or ID, you can have two options regarding utilities:

- Request the service through a special power of attorney if ever you purchase the property under a corporation/ business so that the bill is addressed under the name of the business.

- If you purchase the house under your name, then make sure that before closing the deal the seller/s of the property has already paid all the outstanding utility bills. Make sure to ask for a receipt of all the bills previously paid. Using the receipts/ bills, you'll know whose name it is registered and also the location number which you'll need when transferring the meter under your name.

Communication Services in Costa Rica

The government owned Costa Rican Electricity Institute has now joined with other international and privately owned companies like Claro and Movistar that are the major cell phone service providers. ICE supports GSM and 3G technology, prepaid service is also available. Some internet and cellular service providers are quite new in Costa Rica so you may experience spotty coverage particularly in remote areas. This section will give you an overview of the different communication service providers in Costa Rica as well as their features and rates.

GSM

Services and Rates

- Plans or package deals for GSM are not available as each user pays for minute calls used per month but incoming calls are free of charge.
- Voicemails service, call forwarding and waiting, and conference calls are also free of charge.
- There is an activation charge that costs 12,500 CRC (US$25). Basic account fees usually cost 3,277 CRC (US$6.50) per month inclusive of sales tax and 1 hour of outgoing calls.
- You'll need to pay an additional cost of around 250 CRC every month for Caller IDs.
- SMS or mobile messaging costs 1.70 CRC for a maximum of 160 characters.

- International calls are quite expensive; if you call someone in the U.S. $0.26/ minute.

Claro

Services and Rates

- Claro provides 3G plans that costs anywhere between $20 and $100 per month. It is inclusive of SMS and MMS messages, and calls per minute.
- International calls to US and Canada will cost around 34 CRC per minute.
- The internet speed is 256 kps to 1.5 Mbps for an additional cost of 2,500 to 12,000 CRC (US$5 to S24).
- You can also avail special smartphone plans.

Below are the mobile and internet packages of Claro:

Plan	Calls per Minute	SMS	MMS	Rate

Claro 1	320	500	20	10,000 CRC
Claro 2	500	1000	40	15,000 CRC
Claro 3	700	1300	60	20,000 CRC
Claro 4	950	1500	80	25,000 CRC
Claro 5	2,500	2000	100	50,000 CRC

Kolbi

Services and Rates

- Kolbi also offers 3G services and you can choose from their different packages like the basic package and phone packages. Phone packages may be quite expensive compared to just purchasing a separate phone.

- Activation charge will cost you a 12,500 CRC (US$25)
- Voicemails service, incoming calls, call forwarding and waiting, and conference calls are also free of charge.
- Exceeding calls per minute or calls/services that exceeds your selected plan will have an additional cost of 33.90 CRC for peak times (7 A.M to 7 P.M. Monday thru Fridays); and 25.99 CRC for non – peak times.
- There's an additional cost for both messages and media messaging if you exceed your selected plan. The cost is around 1.70 CRC.

Below are the mobile and internet packages of Kolbi:

Plan	Calls per Minute	SMS	MMS	Rate
Kolbi Basic	60	30	0	3,277 CRC

Kolbi 150	150	350	10	6,485 CRC
Kolbi 250	250	500	15	9,647 CRC
Kolbi 500	500	1,500	25	17,874 CRC
Kolbi 750	750	1,500	30	24, 423 CRC
Kolbi Executive 1,000	1,000	1,000	30	29,903 CRC

Movistar

Services and Rates

- Movistar offers 5 basic cellular plans each including calls/texts per minute, and also minutes to your favorite Movistar number

- Each minute that exceeds your selected plan can have an additional cost anywhere between 25.99 CRC to 33.90 CRC per minute depending on the time of day.
- You can also have the option to add an extra package to you selected plan. An additional of 150 minutes will cost you 3,000 CRC valid for 1 month.
- There are also long distance plans that will cost you around US$5 for 25 minutes of calls to US or Canada.
- The internet speed is up to 1 Mbps only. There are also special packages for iPhones.

Below are the mobile and internet packages of Movistar:

Plan	Calls per Minute	SMS	My Favorite Movistar Minutes	Rate
XS	60	60	60	3,250 CRC
S	250	500	150	9,000 CRC

M	500	1,500	300	17,000 CRC
L	800	1,500	400	24,000 CRC
XL	1,500	1,500	500	34,000 CRC

3G Prepaid

Most providers in Costa Rica such as Claro, Movistar and Kolbi provide 3G prepaid cellular options.

- **Kolbi:** The 3G prepaid services is available for national and international sim chips. National chips can be purchased for increments of 2,500 CRC, 5,000 CRC, and 10,000 CRC. International chips if you want to call in United States cost around 11,400 CRC.

Daytime minute will cost 33.90 CRC, and 25.99 CRC for nighttime and weekend texts, conference calls, caller ID, voicemail, and 911 service. 3G internet and MMS can also be added in your prepaid plan. You can also recharge your minutes through automatic payments or you can also purchase additional minutes at authorized dealers. Additional minutes starts at 50 CRC. You can also purchase prepaid cards where you can enter the pin and code written and load it up yourself.

- **Claro:** Prepaid service costs 2,500 CRC per sim card. You can recharge it or add minutes via online, Claro hotspots or Claro's call centers all over the country. Recharge amount starts at 500 CRC.

  - **Movistar:** The company has its own prepaid service plan that costs around 28 to 34 CRC per minute, and 1.70 CRC per SMS/ MMS. International texts will cost an additional of 85

CRC. The sim card costs around $5, and comes with 2,500 CRC worth of credit.

Chapter Six: Work and Business in Costa Rica

The usual problem when finding a job in Costa Rica if you're a foreigner is that you also need a work permit. Sometimes you need one to get the other. Most companies you'll apply in will ask if you have a working permit but usually you can only get it if you're employer take a chance on you and hire you. Nevertheless, it's best that you first apply for a working permit before formally applying in any job. This chapter will give you information on how you can apply, the requirements you need, and also the procedures.

For many expats, landing a job is quite challenging because the application process can be different from one's home country, but perhaps it's much harder to land a work that will match your qualifications, interests, and financial needs.

This is certainly a big challenge for any newcomer who is still adjusting to the expat life in Costa Rica because it will take some time before you can build your working qualifications and gain a working experience in the country that will hopefully attract the job you want. This chapter will also cover how an expat like you can set up your own business, the permits you need to have, and the process of registering your business. This will all be essential to ensure that you won't break any laws regarding earning money and making a living in Costa Rica

Working in Costa Rica

Before anything else you need to first become a temporary/permanent resident of Costa Rica before applying for a working permit or before attempting to find a job. We've discussed in previous chapters how expats can apply for a temporary/ permanent residence. In order to apply for a working permit you need to prepare the following documents:

- Application Form
- Letter that states why you want to apply for a working permit. The letter should also indicate your name, age, current address (in Costa Rica), nationality, and also the place/means for notification like an email address or contact number.
- Receipt of payment per each page that is attached to the residency application which costs around 125 CRC.
- Birth Certificate
- 2 passport size photographs

- Receipt of finger point registration (as issued by the Ministry of Public Security)
- Receipt of Consular Inscription
- Criminal record from the place you've been living for the last 3 years or in your native country.
- Copy of the migration document to prove that you're a legal resident of the said country (either your native country or where you've been living in the last 3 years).
- Certified copies of passport pages (each page)
- Statement of employing company indicating the function that you'll undertake, the salary and the contract/ duration.
- Legal Constitution and also the registration documents of the company you'll apply in.
- Certification of the Social Security Institution of Costa Rica. This statement will serve as proof the your potential employer/ company is registered and that they have no outstanding monetary obligations.
- Your proof of income, balance, and result as issued by the Public Accountant.

- Insurance company statement indicating that the worker is duly paid.

Depending on where you live in Costa Rica, it may take some time for you to adjust to the working culture. This section will cover everything you need to know about what it's like as a worker in Costa Rica.

Working Hours

There are 2 types of working days in Costa Rica; the *Jornadas Ordinarias Normales* (Normal Working Day) and the *Jornadas Especiales o de Excepcion* Special Working Days. *Jornadas Ordinarias Normales*. Both kinds are divided into day shifts and nightshifts.

Jornadas Ordinarias Normales

- The normal daytime working day is 8 to 10 hours (if the work in not heavy or unhealthy) depending on your company policy or what the work demands.

- The normal daytime office hours are between 5AM and 7 PM.
- Nightshift jobs are between 7 PM and 5 AM.
- Nightshift jobs shouldn't be no more than 6 hours per day or a total of 36 hours per week.
- There is also what they call mixed shifts; this is when an employee works partly during the day and also at night. Nevertheless, the maximum working hour per week for a mixed shift is 42 hours only.

Jornadas Especiales o de Excepcion

Special Working Day is when an employee works during the weekends. It also applies to domestic employees or servants that work for up to 12 hours per day. If that's the case, the domestic helper is entitled to a 1 ½ hour break every day.

Minors who are above 15 years old but below 18 years old are also considered under the Special Working Day. This usually applies to child stars or those young actors. They are not allowed to work for more than 6 hours a day or a total of 36 hours per week otherwise they could violate the working laws.

Wages

Employee salary is lower compared to North American countries and in Europe. This is why you should also compute your cost of living per month to ensure that your job can sustain your monthly expenses. There are also benefits depending on the company you're working for, Christmas bonus (13 month pay), severance package, and also vacation leaves and paid holidays. Overtime is paid as the hourly rate plus 50%. Below is the rate per hour for each kind of work in Costa Rica, this can also be subject to change:

- Non - Qualified Worker: 8.416,72 CRC per hour (US$16)
- Semi - Qualified Worker: 9.164,03 CRC per hour (US$17.2)
- Qualified Worker: 9.340,79 CRC per hour (US$18.60)

- High School level technicians: 303.137,69 CRC per month (US$608.12)
- Specialized Worker: 324.850,54 CRC per month (US$651.68)
- College technicians: 373.583,85 CRC per month (US$749.41)
- Bachelor's Degree: 403.484,51 CRC per month (US$809.39)
- *Licenciatura* Licensed Degree: 549.195,15 CRC per month (US$1101,69)

The salaries stated above cover the following industries/ sectors:

- Agriculture
- Mining
- Manufacturing
- Industry
- Construction
- Electricity
- Commerce
- Tourism

- Services
- Transportation
- Storage

Labor Regulations

Working contracts in Costa Rica can either be written or verbal. Usually, verbal agreement contracts are jobs in the agricultural, domestic service, cattle industry or for temporary jobs that only last for less than 90 days.

There are 2 types of Labor Contracts; Limited Time Contracts, and Unlimited Time Contracts.

Limited Time Contracts: This kind of contracts as the name suggests, indicates a time span or when the work is going to end once it has been performed.

Unlimited Time Contracts: This kind of contract is usually for the long – term and has no specified time span. As long as the company doesn't terminate you, you're most likely going to be renewed for an indefinite time.

- In cases of termination, employees have the right in getting a lay – off compensation. Both the employer and employee are entitled to a 1 month notice before the termination of contracts either via lay – off or if the employee resigns.

- Employees are also entitled for 2 weeks of vacation leave for every 50 weeks of continuous employment. If ever the employee's contract is terminated and he or she hasn't used any earned vacation leave, the employee is entitled to a payment of one day's salary for each month that he or she worked during the year.
- You can avail the Maternity leave for 1 month before the birth of your child, and 3 months after the birth with a fully paid salary.

- Employers pay around 46% tax every year for their employees, and a 22% for their employees Social Security payment.

All employees will also need to pay taxes, and will most likely be a salary deduction. Check the government website at http://dgt.hacienda.go.cr for more information regarding tax periods. Below is the income tax amount you have to pay depending on your salary per month:

- You don't need to pay an income tax if you have a salary of 3,042,000 CRC and below.
- If you have a salary of 3,042,000 CRC to 4,543,000 CRC, you'll pay 10% income tax.
- If you have a salary of 4,543,000 CRC to 7,577,000 CRC, you'll pay 15% income tax.
- If you have a salary of 7,577,000 CRC to 15.185.000 CRC, you'll pay 20% income tax.
- If you have a salary of above 15.185.000 CRC, you'll pay 25% income tax.

Holidays

In Costa Rica there are paid and also unpaid holidays. Paid holidays obviously mean that the employers are obliged to pay in full their employees. Employees also have the right to not go to work or are forced to work during the holidays; if they do, the employer can be fined. However, if the employee agrees to work on holidays, he/she is entitled to a double salary. Below is the list of paid working holidays:

- New Year (January 1)
- Juan Santamaría Day (April 11)
- Jueves y Viernes Santos (Maundy Thursday and Good Friday, during the Holy Week)
- Labor Day (May 1)
- Anexión del partido de Nicoya a Costa Rica (July 25)
- Motherday and Asuncion de la Vírgen (August 15)
- Independence Day (September 15)
- Christmas (December 25)

Non-paid holidays are:

- Virgen of Los Angeles Day (August 22)

- Culture Day (October 12)

Employee Rights and Disputes

If ever your employer has done some form of injustice to you or that your rights are violated in cases of say, non – payment of salary, you can sue them. You can contact the *Inspección Nacional de Trabajo* or the National Work Inspection to file a report or lawsuit.

Doing Business in Costa Rica

Costa Rica is one of the most visited international hotspot in the world. It's a democratic country that has enjoyed peace since the 50's. Even if it's just a small country just covering around 0.03%, it is still home to 5% of the planet's biodiversity. What makes Costa Rica more appealing to tourists is that it also offers a great setting for international brands, and multinational companies to set up businesses and offer various services to both locals and foreigners. It is definitely a great investment location.

The country is a great place for innovative foreigners or expats who would like to create their own startups and take a risk of building new business establishments. Compared to United States and European countries, startup businesses in Costa Rica will just need a lower startup capital. According to the local *Caja Costarricense del Seguro Social* (Social Security System), the number of self – employed individuals in the country has more than doubled over the past few years, which means that Costa Rica is a place of doing business with ease, and opportunities are abundant. Most businesses and companies are largely own by Costa Rican nationals but there's also quite a large percentage of foreigners/ expats who start their businesses in the country.

Another proof that Costa Rica is a great place for budding entrepreneurs, particularly foreign expats is that the country is ranked number one among Latin American countries when it comes to providing protection for private businesses and also commercial freedom. Costa Rica ranks number nine in the world when it comes to doing business with ease.

Expats who are granted with temporary residency are allowed to setup their businesses with only a few restrictions compared to other countries. If you're thinking about where to start, you might want to consider places with a lot of foot traffic. It's wise to do research about the local consumer market. Around 75% of the population resides in major cities like San Jose, Heredia, Cartago, Alajuela, and the Central Valley. These cities are where most of the country's purchasing power can be found, thus a great place to start. The demographic also tells us that Costa Rica has a young population with more than 60% of the people are 30 years old and below. In order for budding foreign entrepreneurs to success, they should be able to adjust to their local market's needs, and perhaps, also cater those who are below the poverty line. According to statistics, only 2 out of 3 businesses setup by expats succeed, if you think you or your business idea got what it takes then take note of the next few sections.

Types of Business Structures in Costa Rica

You can choose different kinds of business structure that best fits your business. Just like in most countries, the different corporate structures are the following:

- General Partnership (*Sociedad en Nombre Colectivo)*
- Limited Liability Company (*Sociedad de Resposibilidad Limitada)*
- Limited Partnership (*Sociedad en Comandita)*
- Limited Company/ Corporation (Sociedad Anonima)

General Partnerships

This type of business structure is owned by partners where both liabilities and also business responsibilities are shared, and their liability is not limited.

Limited Partnerships

This type of business structure is run by a group that directs the company, manages the business, and also represents the shareholder's interests. The liability of the partners is limited to the original declared value of the business. When you set up and register your company, you and your partners should have a written agreement about the rights and duties of one another. All of your partners should be aware if there will be any changes to the agreement, and you'll need to also have a company lawyer. The agreement must stipulate if the partners have equal rights in the company as some may have invested more than others or have put up more capital during the start - up. The largest shareholder will likely have more rights in the company, but all partners are still jointly responsible for all the obligations and potential losses incurred.

Limited Liability Company

This type of business structure is where the liability of the partners is limited only to their original investment in the company. This is pretty much the same with standard partnerships in all respects, but the only difference is that the partners have limited liabilities to pay the debts incurred by other partner/s.

Limited Company/ Corporation

This type of business structure is owned by various shareholders that remain anonymous. *Sociedad Anonima* is usually for big shot companies/businesses that have large capitals, have board of investors, and companies that already has a certain reputation and credibility in the business world.

Naming Your Business

The law stipulates that those who own a Limited

Company/ Corporation should have a unique business name so as not to mistake it with any other name of a company. The company name should also bear the initials of S.A. (Sociedad Anonima) to indicate that the business is incorporated. The company name can be in any language but the firm's charter should have a Spanish translation, The meaning of the company's name should have an explanation to prove that it came from the owner/s themselves.

You or your partners should register the company name under the Registro de Marcas de Comercio, and it should be approved by the organization to copyright the name under you/ your company, and protect it from being used by others.

Acquiring Business Licenses

Once the business structure is formed and you have already registered your business' name, the next step is to apply for a business license or locally known as Patente Municipal from the government office where your business/

company is located in. Do take note of the following when registering your business:

- Ensure that the zone rules in your desired location allow your business or desired activity before you sign any property/ leasing agreement.
- You need to have a signed agreement of your leasing/ property purchase, and it must be initiated before the authorities.
- You should also obtain work risk insurance for your employees from the local insurance agency.
- Your company should register at the Social Security Institution of Costa Rica as an employer.

You should also apply for a health permit at the Ministry of Health after getting a zoning permit approval. Once your health permit is issued/ approved, your business will be formally registered.

Chapter Seven: Family & Education in Costa Rica

Moving with your children in Costa Rica can be quite a lot of work at first, but you can also look forward to having more fun adventures with them. Most foreign expats relocate to Costa Rica because they have sort of this idyllic vision of their kids living a different kind of life, or perhaps a much better life than what they had growing up. The vision of most parents is to provide their children some sense of freedom, and also have that connection with the environment. However, the initial transition is usually tougher and daunting because aside from logistic struggles, most children expats have problems adjusting to the culture and way of living in Costa Rica – not to mention the language.

Culture shock usually comes with the dream of living in a different country, and if you're someone coming from North America, Europe or Asia, you'll immediately see how different the people from South American countries live their lives. There are many opportunities and unique Costa Rican experiences awaiting foreign expats and their families, not to mention the many benefits that permanent residents can take advantage of such as the quality of education, various healthcare benefits, tax breaks, as well as employment and business opportunities. According to various surveys conducted over the past few years, the quality of life is what many immigrants like about relocating in Costa Rica.

This is what you're going to learn in this chapter. This will help you decide if Costa Rica is the country where you want to raise your children and family.

Acclimating Children and Family Living in Costa Rica

Relocating to any country for this matter is both, an adventure, and also an adversity that can easily be solved once you and your family became familiarized with the culture - both the positive and negative – the people, and the overall environment. Acceptance is key when it comes to change. If you allow yourself to learn and absorb everything there is that this new change is offering then it can truly impact your life and that of your family in the long run, and can help you adjust easily. Research is also essential so that you can make informed decisions and act with confidence. These are good traits that you can use when acclimating your children once you make the move to Costa Rica.

Here are some things to keep in mind to ensure a smooth transition for your children:

Language Barriers

Obviously, your children will need to get used to the local language which is Spanish. Learning and practicing the language is essential when it comes to moving to other countries as this will help you and your children in your everyday lives. If you and your family can speak the native tongue, you will be able to easily connect to Costa Ricans, and make friends. It will help you in your day to day life, and will also keep you safe from any fraudulent circumstances. As for your children, it'll most likely be easier for them to grasp the language since most kids still have a sharp mind at this stage of their lives compared to adults.

Once they go to school, they'll get the chance to practice speaking and writing the language, making them immersed and well – versed in Spanish as they grow up. It will be quite difficult at first, so in order to make it easy for your child, it's wise that you enroll them in a bi – lingual public/ private school in Costa Rica where there are subjects in both Spanish and English. In this way, they can slowly learn the new language and not feel intimidated. Another great tip is to get them to learn the basics of the language before you even make the move so that they can already have an idea of how it works.

Environment

If you're someone who have lived in big cities or the metropolis with little to no natural sceneries around, it can be another issue when it comes to acclimating your children in Costa Rica since they're not used to this kind of rural lifestyle. As a parent, it's all a matter of showing them that this country is like one huge playground where they can truly enjoy. What most expat parents do once they have already settled in their new home is to go out for a family trip. This is a great way to introduce Costa Rica to your kids. Let them see the beauty that the country has to offer.

As you now know, Costa Rica is home to the most exotic faunas and floras. It boasts many crystal clear beaches, and stunning landscapes that anyone can enjoy, and it's a country that will surely feel like one big adventure. Take them out and do outdoor activities with them. Immerse them with their new environment, introduce them to the culture, socialize with the locals, and let them also be aware of how they can stay safe and how to properly take care of the environment so that they'd grown up as responsible citizens.

Food

Another major factor that makes it difficult for expat kids to adjust is the food. There are many international cuisines/ restaurants in the country, and most brand of foods are also available in huge grocery outlets but if you want your children to really be one of the Costa Ricans, they have to know how to eat local foods as some types of meals found in North America or Europe may not always be available especially if you live in rural areas. The best way is to already introduce Costa Rican food to them before you make the move just so they won't be shocked to the food choices in the country.

The staple meal in Costa Rica often includes beans, rice and a casado (set meal). It usually includes veggies and meat, and if you'll be residing along the coast, then you can expect to always have a fresh supply of seafood. Some kids are still picky at this stage and most of them will only eat cheese sandwich or mac and cheese which is also available but it's still best that you introduce them to the local cuisine as this is part of their transition. What you can do though is to keep a stock in the kitchen of their favorite foods/ imported products from your home country to make it easier for them.

Safety

Costa Rica is a very safe country compared to other countries in Central America. Rarely would you hear any news about violence or crimes in the country. It's extremely safe and it's also the reason why lots of expats especially those with children don't have doubts coming and residing here. Hate crimes and other forms of extreme violence are usually unheard of. This doesn't mean though that there aren't any crimes, it's just that it's very low and insignificant. You won't also find riots/ rallies or forms of protests because the government is stable, and it's generally a peaceful and nature loving country. This is how Costa Rica earned its nickname as the "Switzerland of the Americas."

Of course, no country is totally immune to global crime rates. Petty crimes still occur but the good news is that most of it is property – related or business related. If you abandon your house for a long time, and you didn't hire anyone to take care of it while you're away, chances are that someone will broke into it and stay there until they get caught. The usual "crimes" is also in the form of pickpocketing especially to tourists, so never leave your things unattended or your house/ vehicle unlocked.

It's also wise that you don't show off too much or act like you're some very rich person – even if you are, it's best to keep a low profile so that you won't attract any intruders or robbers. If you're going around town or in unfamiliar places, just wear casual clothes, less jewelry or other flashy things, don't bring lots of cash, and don't show off your gadgets too much. Always be mindful of your belongings, and alert especially if you're in an unfamiliar territory. Don't also leave any items outside your home or backyard where robbers can easily get it. Make sure that everything is lock when you leave and better yet install a security system like a CCTV in your house especially if you're not around all the time.

Expat Communities

Costa Rica is increasingly becoming a hotspot not just for tourists but also for expatriates particularly those from United States, and Canada since it is just close to their native homes. Once you get here, you can see many North American influences.

This is a great thing because it means that you and your family can easily find expat communities that can help you in adjusting to your new life. There are many large and well – connected expat neighborhoods in many major cities in the country. There are even local programs that aim to help newcomers in acclimating to the new culture. You can also find different expat groups or social clubs in sports, hobbies, and other gatherings. However, the downside to this is that too much exposure to the expat community may make you miss the whole point of why you relocated in the first place – to immerse in the local culture/ environment.

This is why it's highly recommended that you first decide what level of expat community you and your family are after. Yes, it's nice to see fellow natives around because they'll make you feel at home and can definitely guide you and help you in your first few months of residing in Costa Rica but you also would want to have the opportunity to immerse yourself in the authentic Costa Rican experience, so better choose your tolerance level for expats beforehand.

What most expats do is that they live in areas where there are few expats in the community, and they just sort of reach out to other fellow natives through attending weekly/ monthly expat gatherings. Some expats prefer to not have any fellow countrymen around so that they'll be force to really get to know the locals and the Costa Rican way of life

– away from the hustle and bustle of North American influences. However, it's still important that before you make any decision, you first consult and also consider the needs of your family.

School Options and Education Systems in Costa Rica

The education system in Costa Rica has dramatically improved over the last few years. The country's adult literacy rate have also improved; reaching around 95%, thanks to the upgraded school systems in both South and Central America.

Public Schools

Public education in Costa Rica is mandatory and also free but usually only offered in Spanish. Every child between the ages of 6 and 13 should attend primary school. High school or secondary school is voluntary. Most children in Costa Rica attend 6 years of primary school, and around 5 to 6 years of high school depending if the student will attend an academic school or a technical school. Usually the first 3 years of secondary education will cover general topics like Science, Math, Economics, History, Spanish/ English (in private schools), while the remaining 2 to 3 years will focus on specialize fields.

Once the student completes their secondary education, he/she will receive a diploma in either arts or sciences or also known as Bachillerato Diploma. Students will need this to qualify for a college education and attend a Costa Rican university. Completing a degree in secondary school and even in college may not be enough if you're kid decides to enroll in schools/universities abroad; some subjects may be credited but not all. This goes the same when enrolling your children in a Costa Rican school. The completed levels done outside the country may not be sufficient to get your kid to the next level so check the school's requirements/ qualification. If this is the case, then your children will need to go back to the same level.

Private Schools

Most private schools in the country have their own set of curriculum and some of which may even follow the school system of the United States. There are also lots of private schools that offer students the opportunity to study for an International Baccalaureate Diploma/ U.S. High School Diploma. However, most private schools are located in the capital of San Jose and the Guanacaste region, and may not be common in rural regions.

School Regulations

Before enrolling your children in a Costa Rican school, whether public or private, the school will need your legal proof of residency/ residency visa, transcripts from the previous school and other important documents like birth certificate, diploma (if any), etc. Ask the school of your choice regarding the requirements.

- The school year begins in February and ends in December. There'll also be around 2 months of vacation during summer time and also the coffee picking season. Dates can vary but usually students were given 2 weeks off around July, during the Holy Week (April), and other public holidays like Thanksgiving and Christmas.

- A typical school day starts at 7 am until around 2 to 3 pm in the afternoon with recess and lunch breaks in between.

- The average students per classroom are around 30, and all schools require students to wear the prescribed uniforms.

- Most public schools don't offer extracurricular activities so if you want your child to experience different sports and other opportunities then it's best that you enroll him/ her in private schools.

Universities and Colleges

You can choose to enroll in public and private universities. When it comes to enrollment, it can be quite competitive to secure a slot in particular courses or degrees. Non – residents or expats will need to have a student visa or a residency visa in order for you to attend a university. This goes the same for those expats who wanted to continue their studies here. Public universities usually offer Spanish classes, but there are also lots of English classes that are available by request especially if you're a non – resident.

Private universities also offer full English courses and language degree courses.

The tuition fees of most public and private universities cost anywhere between US$2,500 to $3,000 per year for undergraduate courses. If you're going to study for a post – graduate degree, it will cost around $4,000 for tuition fee alone. These rates are still relatively lower compared to American and European universities. The most regarded university in the country is the University of Costa Rica.

Chapter Eight: Taxes & Banking in Costa Rica

Lots of North American citizens come to the great coast of Costa Rica to start a new life or simply enjoy what the Caribbean has to offer in terms of quality living. When it comes to taxes, Costa Rica is known as the "Switzerland of the Americas" because the country is a tax haven for foreigners residing here. If you're an professional employee or skilled worker, you'll have to pay the income tax. If you own a real estate or business, you'll pay a property tax or a corporation tax. Even if you're already retired or just someone looking to stay in the country, one way or another you'll have to incur certain taxes every time you pay for goods or avail services.

As an expat the rules for paying taxes in Costa Rica, and the amount will be quite different and probably even less than what you pay in your home country. This is also advantageous for people who'll be doing business in the country because they can possibly minimize their tax obligations. It's highly recommended that you consult a tax specialist or accountant so that you'll have an idea on how the process works. With their professional advice, you can choose the best option when it comes to declaring taxes for you as an individual expat or for your business.

This chapter will cover important things you need to know when it comes to paying your taxes as a (future) Costa Rican and also an American since there are still US expat tax laws you need to pay. This section will also cover the Costa

Rican Tax System, its overview, and the importance of tax planning so that you'll have a guide on what to do and prepare it before you make your move.

Taxation in Costa Rica

Officially known as the Republic of Costa Rica, it has both a presidential and parliamentary forms of government. The Ministerio de Hacienda (Ministry of Finance) is the federal tax authority in the country that oversees both local and international tax matters as well as the collection, dealings, and tax assessments.

Taxable Income and Rates

Once you have become a Costa Rican resident or have been granted a temporary/ permanent residency visa, as what we've discussed in previous chapter, you'll be obliged to pay income generated taxes. If you own a property, you'll also have to pay a property tax to your local municipality where the property is located, the good news is that there's no capital gains tax.

The taxable income of expats will be based on the net income. According to Costa Rican laws, gross incomes is define as the total amount of income, which also includes profits you've earn in the country as well as profits from your real estate property, businesses, and other investments made during the taxable year. Any increase in net worth is also taxable especially those that cannot be justified by your declared household/ business income.

The table below will show you the tax brackets and rates for those who have are monthly income earners.

Tax Band	Taxable Income	Tax Rate
Basic Allowance/ Salary	792,000 CRC (approx.US$1,415)	Exempted
1st Band	792,000 CRC to	10%

	1,888,000.00 CRC (approx.US$2,124)	
2nd Band	Over 1,888,000.00 CRC (approx. over US$2,124)	15%

Deductions and Exclusions

Costa Rica wouldn't be called the Switzerland of Central America if there aren't any deductions or tax exclusions. Examples of tax exclusions are the following:

- Donations (cash or in kind)
- Reevaluated Fixed Assets
- Depreciable Assets
- Lottery Prizes
- Government Approved Charitable Donations
- Community Properties
- Inheritances
- Profits that are credited to the international incomes, tax payer, and capital gains which are obtained from the retail property sale.

Such deductions are subtracted from the gross income. However, for it to be allowed, the tax payer should be able to prove that the costs incurred are necessary to produce income. Below is a list of taxable income costs.

- Services
- Raw materials
- Parts or components bought to create an income
- Paid out salaries by the tax payer
- Taxes paid on behalf of the products and services produced
- Insurance premiums
- Interest/ bad debts
- Travel expenses (as long as it represents 1% or less of the gross income)
- Advertising costs
- Gifts made to the state
- Startup Costs

Tax Credits

There are 2 types of tax credits in the country that can be paid from one's monthly income.

Tax Credit #1:

For each of the resident's dependents either under 18 years of age, or a high school/ college student below 25 years old or a mentally/ physically ill dependent that is otherwise cannot make it on their own to find a job or make a living, you the tax payer are entitled to 560 CRC tax credit every month, and a 1,800 CRC tax credit every year for each of your dependent that meets the criteria mentioned above.

Tax Credit #2:

If the residents are married to a spouse and are not legally separated, there is a tax credit of 830 CRC every month, and it can also be deducted by one of the 2 married people.

Social Security

Every employee in Costa Rica is obliged to pay a percentage to their social security through salary deductions, and their employers must also pay a certain percentage for each of the social security of their employees as established by law. Below is the table of the social security deductions that'll be subtracted from your salary:

Government Service	**% of Employee**	**% of Employer**
Medical and Maternity	5.50%	9.25%
Disability, Old Age, and Death Benefits	2.84%	5.08%
Complementary Pension	0.00%	0.50%
Family Welfare Programs	0.00%	5.00%

Workmen's Savings Bank	1.00%	0.50%
Labor capitalization fund	0.00%	3.00%
IMAS – Institute of Social Welfare	0.00%	0.50%
INS- National Institute of Securities	0.00%	1.00%
INA – National Institute of Learning	0.00%	1.50%
Total Deductions:	**9.34%**	**26.33%**

Value Added Tax

Locally known as sales tax, this is what consumers pay for every goods and services in the country except medicinal products. It is levied both at the importation and at the point of sale.

Tax Filing

The Costa Rican fiscal year starts in October 1 to September 30. You should pay and file your taxes before February 15 for the year prior to that.

Foreign Taxes and Tax Planning

If you're a temporary/ permanent resident and you're also an expat, your worldwide income is untaxed. For American citizens, Costa Rica and the U.S. have an agreement to share tax information even if they don't have a tax treaty. When it comes to tax planning for U.S. citizens or expats, they are required to submit a U.S. income tax return. There's a foreign tax credited that is allowed for income made in Costa Rica, but it must still reflect on your U.S. income tax return. It's also very likely that expats who works in Costa Rica won't pay any US Income taxes.

Financial Institutions and Banking in Costa Rica

This section will provide you with information regarding banking and opening an account. If you are considering in starting a business or residing in Costa Rica for a period of time, this will be essential. Your immigration status in Costa Rica and the purpose of opening a bank account or other types of account is your main criteria when it comes to deciding which banks you'll best be dealing with.

If you're a legal resident with a valid status, then it'll be very easy to open any type of account, on the other hand, if you're not yet legally approve, the bank/s will decide whether they'll allow you to have an account or not. There are some banks that won't let non – residents open bank accounts, and there are some that will. Other expats who non – residents can also open a bank account using a Costa Rican corporation but it will still depend on the bank if they'll allow it, and if you'll be able to provide the requirements that'll be set by them.

There are many government – owned banks, and also privately owned banks in the country. See the list of banks under each category below:

Government owned banks/ institutions:

- Banco de Costa Rica
- Banco Nacional de Costa Rica
- Banco Crédito Agrícola de Cartago Banco de Costa Rica
- Banco Popular y de Desarollo Comunal

Private Banks:

- Banco BCT S.A.
- Banco Cathay de Costa Rica S.A.
- Banco Davivienda (Costa Rica) S.A.
- Banco de Soluciones Bansol de Costa Rica S.A.
- Banco General (Costa Rica) S.A.
- Banco Improsa S.A.
- Banco Lafise S.A.
- Banco Promérica de Costa Rica S.A.
- Scotiabank de Costa Rica S.A.
- Banco Bac San Jose, S.A.

Regardless of which bank you choose, you'll most likely hear lots of complaints from expats for various reasons. The main reason is that most foreigners are accustomed to a certain level of customer service and easy banking operation in their native countries, and because of this it forms a comparison to the services given by a local bank which often results in frustration. Most American and European banks don't impose their customers a lot of requirement and sort of scrutiny compared to local Costa Rican banks, but that's the way it is, just comply with the rules, and submit all the needed requirements and act accordingly.

If you will be residing in a rural area, the best banks are Banco Nacional and Banco de Costa Rica. They also have many branches. These 2 banks have the best online payment system in the country so that you can pay your taxes, utility bill, and other payments with ease. However, don't be surprised if you need to personally go there for some reason as these banks usually have long lines and poor customer service as what most expats described.

Bank Requirements for Individuals and Corporations

The requirements for each bank will vary and will also depend on your status and the type of account you'd want to open. Generally, most banks will need you to submit the following documents:

- Copy of your passport or residency card
- Reference letter from your current bank.
- Reference letter from account holder (some banks only)

- Tax return (some banks only)
- 12 months of banking statements (some banks only)
- Copy of your utility bill (required by all banks)
- Copy of the deed if ever you own any real estate property (some banks only)
- Know Your Customer Form (required by all banks)

General Requirements for Corporations

If you'd like to open an account under the name of a business or corporation, you'll need to provide these additional requirements:

- Certificate of corporate standing
- Certification of disclosure of shareholders of the corporation
- Certified Public Account statement of income or projected income
- Cash flow statement signed by corporate officer and C.P.A.
- Copy of the bylaws of the corporation

Chapter Nine: Retirement and Healthcare in Costa Rica

"Pura Vida" or Pure Life is the official motto of Costa Rica. This is also something that most expats hope to achieve especially if they choose to retire here. It's usually among the lines of having a simple and good life. What most retirees love about Costa Rica are their all year round great tropical climate and fantastic weather, the quiet urban and rural areas, the mountains, waterfalls, beaches, forests and other wonderful biodiversity that only the country can offer.

According to the United States Department of State, there are around 20,000 plus American retired expats that are now living in Costa Rica and it's because the country has one of the highest standard when it comes to the quality of living in all of Central America.

The economy is growing, the tourism is continuously attracting more people from all over the world, and the country generally caters to everything that tourists and expats need. There are also excellent healthcare services and lower tax payments. This is why it's no wonder that Costa Rica is a great destination for those who want to have a great time in spending their twilight years.

Most expats choose to live in the capital city of San Jose and around the Central Valley because it's in close proximity to many major facilities like international airports, shopping malls, high – end restaurants and hotels as well as top medical facilities and services. This chapter will give you an idea of what it's like in retiring in Costa Rica as well as the health services you can avail.

Retiring to Costa Rica

More and more expats from all over the world consider retiring in Costa Rica for various reasons. However, you do need to take note that for you to qualify as a resident; you need to have a pension of US$1,000 per month to show the Costa Rican government that you and your dependent/s can afford the cost of living in the country.

The cost of living in most Central American countries like Costa Rica is very cheap compared to if you're going to retire in North American countries like Canada or in Europe. Your money will have more buying power and you can live a very comfortable lifestyle especially if you earn more than US$1,000.

What most future expat retirees in Costa Rica likes is the healthcare system in the country. The country offers a lot of great health care options like the latest medical technologies, top – notch doctors, great facilities, and also a high – quality of medical care. Perhaps next to taxes, health care is the reason why the country attracts many foreigners. Many expats especially those above 50 years old consider retiring in Costa Rica because of high quality health care options and at a very low cost at least compared to their native country.

Most retired foreigners who chose to reside in Costa Rica finds that there are also many good quality hospitals, clinics, and pharmacies all over the country even in rural areas. Costa Rica is ranked number 36 best health care in the world according to the World Health Organization (WHO). Regardless of the kind of medical treatment you need, rest assured that Costa Rica's health care system got you covered.

Health Care System in Costa Rica

The health care system in Costa Rica, which is quite unrecognized by many expats, is called Caja Costarricense de Seguro Social (CCSS). It is usually referred to as Caja, and it is run by the government. The system is cost – effective and because of this it can create a longer waiting period to accommodate your medical needs (treatments/ procedures) especially if your condition in non – life threatening. The main advantage though in availing the CCSS is that most hospitals and clinics in Costa Rica accepts CCSS but it's also wise to avail a health care insurance from a private company if you want a quicker service.

In order for you to have access to the open health care system of Costa Rica (CCSS), you should again first have proof of legal residence. If you are, then you can enjoy regular check – ups, low cost surgical procedures, top – notch treatments, and also free pharmaceutical drugs.

You can also avail another health care system called Instituto de Seguro Nacional or INS. This is a health insurance plan that will cover citizens/ residents if the person stays within the network of hospitals, clinics, or doctors covered.

The CCSS and INS are the 2 options for locals and expats alike when it comes to health care. It's up to you if you would like to avail these options or if you wanted to get your own health insurance plan from a private company as a good insurance policy can surely provide additional benefits that are best fitted to your needs.

Private Healthcare for Costa Rican Expats

Private healthcare companies in the country allows patients to both pay in cash and also use their insurance plan to cover the cost of medical treatments. Health care costs in Costa Rica is much cheaper compared to other countries, and you can most likely pay it in cash but it's still wise that before you make the move, you have already invested in a good health insurance plan so that you're medical coverage is guaranteed should anything unfortunate happens to your health.

Below is the comparison of the medical procedures if done in Costa Rica and in countries like the United States. We've also shown here how much you can save in terms of medical treatments/ procedures:

Medical Procedures	Cost in Costa Rica	Cost in United States	Savings in Percentage
Heart Bypass	Approx. $24,000	Approx. $130,000	70 to 80%
Angioplasty	Approx. $9,000	Approx. $57,000	70 to 80%
Heart Valve Replacement	Approx. 15,000	Approx. 160,000	80 to 90%
Hip Replacement	Approx. $12,000	Approx. $43,000	60 to 70%
Knee Replacement	Approx. $11,000	Approx. $40,000	60 to 70%
Spinal Fusion	Approx. $25,000	Approx. $62,000	50 to 60%
Hysterectomy	Approx. $4,000	Approx. $20,000	70 to 80%

US Health Care Cost vs. Costa Health Care Cost

- It will cost you approximately 1/3 more of the healthcare cost in Costa Rica if the procedure will be done in United States or even in Canada.

- The health care system in the country is ranked among the top 3 health care system in Latin America.

- Surgical procedures like bariatric surgery to cure diabetes are not available in the U.S. or Canada. In Costa Rica, Clinica Biblica which offers a bariatric surgery is also one of the top 10 best for this specific medical procedure.

- Even if the medical treatments and procedures are significantly lower, it's still best that you avail or invest in a health insurance policy to ensure that you won't use up all your savings.

Pharmacies and Medicines

Pharmacies in the country are locally known as "Farmacies." These pharmacies can be found all over the country. Most medicines for all sorts of illnesses are usually available, except maybe in other rural or remote areas. If the medicine is not in stock, you can also request and order it. Regulations for antibiotics and other psychotropic drugs are quite less restrictive than in North American countries or in Europe.

Hospitals and Emergency Services

There are lots of great hospitals and medical facilities in Costa Rica. However, you might get to see that some of them, particularly in the rural areas, are still quite unfinished and/or undergoing some form of renovation. Both locals and foreigners will be treated even if you're a tourist. There are also lots of medical facilities in the country that offers various medical services in the fields of pediatrics, gynecology, urology, psychology, general and special surgeries, and other medical fields. There are also facilities targeted to accommodate chiropractors, therapists, acupuncturists, and naturopaths so you're very well covered.

When it comes to emergency services, the hotline is 911. The operator will connect you to the police, fire department or other emergency services/ hospitals. Ambulance services in the country are relatively quick in responding, and their paramedics are also well – trained.

Chapter Ten: Preparing for Your Relocation in Costa Rica

When relocating to another country, it's usually much easier and also cheaper to just sell all your unnecessary belongings and move on; after all you can easily buy those things once you've already settled. Costa Rica's climate may not suit your previous furniture, and some of your appliances may not work in the country due to different kinds of circuits.

Making a move to another country especially if it's very far from your own can be really stressful for most people which is why it's best that you already start packing things up if you're already decided, and if you're now just waiting for the approval of your residency. Every immigrant's situation is different, keep in mind that the list and tips provided here is only an indication of the things you need to do at different stages. Some of the items may not be relevant to your situation but preparation is essential in making a successful transition.

There are many aspects when relocating to a foreign country; this pre – moving checklist will guide you at the different planning stage of your relocation. This chapter will focus on all the most important things you need to consider before you move in to Costa Rica. This is a practical checklist for you and your family so that you'll know what to do, and will have enough time to take care of your unique situations, and so that you won't miss out anything. When it comes to relocating all your things, careful planning and timeline is very important so better start early and better do it right!

Pre – Moving Tips

6 months before Moving

- **Do an "onsite inspection."** Before considering what things you should or shouldn't bring, it's wise to first do your own research. You can do this by taking a quick trip to the country.

- **Set a realistic moving date:** Even if you don't know yet when your application/s will be approved, it's best that you have a target moving date already. You can estimate it once you've already filed your residency application.

- **Create a plan:** Now that you've set the target date, you can then proceed on creating a plan or a set of the things you should do according to priority. Make sure to also set a date for each and check off the items as you complete them.

- **Put your house on sale:** It's best to sell it before you make the move so that you can still organize the paper work that needs to be done. If it sells fast, then ensure that you have an agreement with the new owners on the moving date. If you aren't at least 50% sure you're going to get approved then it's probably best to just wait.

- **De - clutter:** It's now time to start returning the items you've borrowed, and think about the things that are not necessary to bring in your new home. If you can de – clutter early, you'll have time to give it away or properly distribute it.

3 to 4 months before Moving

- **Prep the documents:** At this point, you should start gathering all the important documents that you and your family need. Documents like birth certificates, marriage certificate, police clearances, bank statements etc. will most likely need some time to acquire so better start getting them. Most documents will have 3 to 6 months of validity so better check the Costa Rica immigration website regarding this. You don't want to get your documents too early as it can expire before you go to the country which makes it useless. It's also best that you update your will (if any) or sort out everything you need with your lawyer (if any). You can also renew your driver's license as you'll need it to obtain a new one in Costa Rica.

- **Update the people:** You should also now start creating a list of the people you'll need to inform regarding your move. You can now start cancelling your subscription services and informing your bank. Start signing up for online payments to ensure that the transactions you'll make will have no glitch.

2 to 3 months before Moving

- **Start the garage sale:** Once you've already de - clutter some stuff you can now start packing up the things that you'll bring but are not for daily use. You'll find out later on that there are still some things you can get rid of so why not start selling some of it through a garage sale? Take as little stuff as you can so that you won't have trouble when it comes to shipping them.

- **Health care:** This is now the time to take your final trips to your physician and dentist. Ensure that you've updated your vaccinations, and acquire all the medical records you'll need. Have a copy of your prescriptions so that you can easily present it at any pharmacy in Costa Rica.

- **Search the services:** You can then check out the services near your target area so that once you get there you'll know where to go. Check where the gym is, the school, the stores, the church, and other essential amenities you'll need.

1 to 2 months before Moving

- **Finalize Your Moving Plans:** At this point you can now tell exactly when you're going to move. You can now select a place where you'll live (if you still haven't bought/ rented a place beforehand). Make sure that you've already sealed the deal with the landlord/ seller and have informed them of your moving date.

- **Contact an international moving company:** If in case you'll need to ship some stuff, then it is best that you contact a reliable moving company ahead of time.

- **Check all your documents again:** Ensure that all your documents and that of your kids and even pets (if any) are all available.

- **Set up your communication services:** Ensure that your mailing address is redirected. Update your accounts as well as emails. Inform your phone/ internet providers about your move. Start cancelling utility services, pay up all your debts and utility bills if you have any.

1 to 2 weeks before Moving

- **Overhaul your house:** Recheck if you've got everything sorted out already from your personal belongings to your utilities and other house services you have had. You also want to make sure that you clean the house before you leave especially if another person/family is also moving in it.

- **Finalize your travel details:** Have your residency documents, passports, and other important papers ready. Ensure that you'll have an itinerary once you arrive like where you'll stay (if you haven't settled where to live yet), how you can acquire cash, and other important things that the immigration of Costa Rica will need you to do once your arrive.

Basic Travel Essentials

Residing in Costa Rica is something that most expats look forward to especially after they have retired from their work. Foreigners like the idea of living in a tropical country especially those who came from cold – climate continents, the idea of immersing oneself into a new culture, meeting new people, and engaging in various outdoor activities. The laid back type of living is truly something that all of us want, and Costa Rica is one of the best countries in the world to go to not to mention all the other great advantages that can come with it like a lower cost of living, more natural setting, tax advantages, affordable health care, and the quiet serene way of living. We hope you learned a lot by reading this book. Never stop learning! This chapter will cover some of the travel essentials you may need before relocating to Costa Rica. We also provided important highlight that you need to remember in this book.

Costa Rica Basic Essentials

Here's a quick run – down of the basic essentials when travelling to Costa Rica:

- **Capital City:** San Jose
- **Population: 4,953,199** (as of 2018)
- **Government:** Democratic
- **Current Leader:** Luis Guillermo Solís
- **Religion:** 70.5% Roman Catholics; 38% Evangelical protestants; 11.3% no religion
- **Currency:** Costa Rican Colon (CRC/ ₡)
- **Language:** Spanish; English

- **Electricity:** 110 Volts (60 hertz), similar to U.S. plugs; 2 pronged flat type.
- **ATMs/Money:** Visa, Master Card, American Express are widely accepted; traveller's cheques and foreign currencies are also accepted in major shops/restaurants

- **General Entry Requirements:**
    - Valid Passport
    - Tourist Visa/ Residence Visas/Permits
    - Return Tickets
    - Hotel bookings/reservations
    - Other travel documents (bank statements; proof of sufficient funds etc.)

- **Climate:** Sunny and humid weather all year round. Occasional rainfalls and has an average temperature of 70 to 81 degrees Fahrenheit in most places in the country.

- **Tipping:** at least 5 – 10% tip for local waiters/bars/restaurants if service charge is not yet included. At least 10 – 15% if you are dining in international establishments. Of course, this higly depends on you but most locals don't tip.

- **Communication:**
    - **To make calls in Costa Rica and the USA:** You need to dial 00 followed by the Country Code (US/ Canada: 1; U.K.: 44, Australia: 61). After doing that you can then dial the area code and number (8 digits).

Quick Summary

General Overview: Costa Rica is one of the most peaceful countries in Central America which is great for potential expats. It's also the only country without an army or military.

Location: It is near Nicaragua and Panama. Have ports in the Caribbean Sea and Pacific Ocean.

Country Capital: San José

Population: Men: 49.86%; Female: 50.14%

Density: 203 inhabitants per sq. mile

Government: Constitutional Government

Languages Spoken: Spanish and English

Longevity: Most Costa Ricans have an average life expectancy of 75 years.

Environmental Diversity: Due to its geographical location, Costa Rica is filled with fauna and flora. You'll find many mangrove observation spots, fauna, and amazing landscapes which are picture – perfect.

Habitat: lowland jungles to arid bare mountain peaks

Literacy Rate: 96. 2%

Public Health Services Coverage: 90% of the population

Health Expenditures: 27.8% of government total

Highest Point: Mount Chirripó

Geography and Climate

- The dry season starts around December and lasts until April.
- You can expect a very hot climate. It usually starts around March to April.
- The cooler dry season starts around November to January since trade winds flow through the mountain around this time.
- The dry season also brings temperature fluctuations and can vary from 14 to 18 degrees in its days and nights.
- The rainy season starts in the month of May until the first few weeks of November.
- You can expect a warm mornings and mild to heavy showers in the afternoon around July to August. Heavy downpours usually occur from September to October.

Temporary Residency Immigration Program

- Pensionado (Retiree): The minimum pension required is US$1,000 per month, and that includes your spouse and dependents (if any) in your application

- Rentista (Income Recipient): It will require you to prove that you have a monthly income of US$2,500. This amount will also include your spouse and any of your children under the age of 25 years old as they will serve as your dependents.

- Investor (Inversionista): It will require you to make an investment. The minimum investment is US$200,000. Once approved, it will include your spouse and any of your children under the age of 25 years old as they will serve as your dependents.

Supporting Documents for Application of Residency

- Birth Certificate
- Police Clearance Certificate
- Marriage Certificate
- Proof of Income Source
- Copy of Your Passport
- Registration with your local Embassy
- Photographs
- Power of Attorney
- Hoja de Filiacion

- Application Fee: The application fee in Costa Rica will cost you US$50. You also have to pay Colones ₡125 plus 2.50 per page of the application (government filing fee). You might also pay US$200 if you wish to change your status.

- Application Duration: You can expect to wait around 7 to 15 months. Average waiting time is 12 months or 1 year.

District for Expats Overview

Puerto Jimenez

Quick Facts:

- **Area:** Osa Peninsula
- **Avg. Temperature:** 27° C
- **Landscape:** Mostly beaches and tropical rainforests
- **Activities:** Wildlife tours, kayak riding, fishing, outdoor adventures

- **Attractions:** Golfo Dulce, Corcovado National Park, Osa, Wildlife Sanctuary, Playa Puntarenitas, Cabo Matapalo
- **Nearby Airports:** Juan Santa Maria Int'l Airport, Puerto Jimenez Airstrip
- **Public Transportation:** Frequent bus service to and from the area of Matapalo and from San Jose
- **Stores:** There are lots of small markets nearby, various food stands, local shops, and restaurants
- **ATMs:** Yes
- **Banks:** No
- **Schools:** No
- **Gas Stations:** Yes
- **Wi – Fi/ Mobile Coverage:** Most areas have a coverage though signal may vary. Has a reliable connection
- **Medical Facilities:** Has small clinics but the nearest hospital is a boat ride away

Golfito

Quick Facts:

- **Best for:** Families, solo travelers, adventure seekers, nature lovers
- **Public Transportation:** very accessible; has many public buses, and taxi boats are also available
- **Stores:** There are lots of groceries, stores, shops and boutiques
- **ATMs:** Yes and there are also several banks
- **Gas Stations:** Yes
- **Wi – Fi/ Mobile Coverage:** Has a reliable connection; most restaurants and coffee shops have coverage
- **Medical Facilities:** Has public hospitals; private clinics and also a couple of pharmacies
- **Attractions:** Piedras Blancas National Park, Playa Zacundo, Playa Payones, Playa Cabo Matapalo
- **Activities:** Trekking, surfing, scuba diving, kayaking, snorkeling, swimming, bird watching, sports fishing, mountain biking, horse riding, whale/ dolphin watching

Cartago

- **Area:** Central Valley & Highlands
- **Avg. Temperature:** 25° C
- **Landscape:** Valleys; elevated landscapes
- **Activities:** white water rafting, trekking, leisure tours in National parks and botanical gardens, hiking
- **Attractions:** Irazu Volcano, Our Lady of the Angels Basilica, Reventazon River, Lankester Botanical Gardens, Savegre Reserve, Chirripo National Park
- **Nearby Airports:** Tobias Bolanos International Airport
- **Public Transportation:** Regular buses from and to San Jose; has limited shuttle buses to nearby attractions
- **Stores:** There are lots of small markets nearby, various food stands, local shops, and restaurants
- **ATMs:** Yes
- **Banks:** Yes
- **Schools:** Yes
- **Gas Stations:** Yes

- **Wi – Fi/ Mobile Coverage:** Most areas have a coverage though signal may vary. Has a reliable connection
- **Medical Facilities:** Max Peralta Jimenez Hospital, Cartago

Puntarenas

- **Area:** Central Pacific
- **Avg. Temperature:** 33° C
- **Landscape:** Beach and port
- **Activities:** surfing, scuba diving, boat cruises, windsurfing, canopy tours
- **Attractions:** Puntarenas Marine Park, Museo Historico Marino (Marine History Museum), La Casa de la Cultura Art Gallery, Tortuga Island, Carara National Park, Penas Biancas National Park
- **Nearby Airports:** Florencia Airport
- **Public Transportation:** regular buses to Jaco, intercity bus service, ferry ride to Nicoya Peninsula

- **Stores:** There are lots of outdoor markets nearby, various food stands, local shops, and souvenir vendors
- **ATMs:** Yes
- **Gas Stations:** Yes
- **Wi – Fi/ Mobile Coverage:** Most areas have a coverage though signal may vary. Has a reliable connection
- **Medical Facilities:** Costa Rica Social Security System Hospital

Cost of Living

Average Cost per Month: If you're the kind of person who lives a simple lifestyle, and only cares for your daily duties, you can budget around US$1,500 more or less per month.

Housing Costs: Renting a place in most rural and urban areas can cost anywhere between US$300 and $600.

Food and Dining: Local meal: $2 to $4; Premium or imported goods will cost you a minimum of $200 or more for a 1 week worth of groceries.

Goods, Services and Entertainment: You can hire a housekeeper and it will only cost you US$2 per hour; when it comes to entertainment, going to museums and cultural establishment tickets usually cost $5 per person.

Health Care: Medical insurances costs around US$60 to $150 per month

Working Requirements:

- Application Form
- Letter that states why you want to apply for a working permit. The letter should also indicate your name, age, current address (in Costa Rica), nationality, and also the place/means for notification like an email address or contact number.
- Receipt of payment per each page that is attached to the residency application which costs around 125 CRC.
- Birth Certificate
- 2 passport size photographs
- Receipt of finger point registration (as issued by the Ministry of Public Security)

- Receipt of Consular Inscription
- Criminal record from the place you've been living for the last 3 years or in your native country.
- Copy of the migration document to prove that you're a legal resident of the said country (either your native country or where you've been living in the last 3 years).
- Certified copies of passport pages (each page)
- Statement of employing company indicating the function that you'll undertake, the salary and the contract/ duration.
- Legal Constitution and also the registration documents of the company you'll apply in.
- Certification of the Social Security Institution of Costa Rica. This statement will serve as proof the your potential employer/ company is registered and that they have no outstanding monetary obligations.
- Your proof of income, balance, and result as issued by the Public Accountant.
- Insurance company statement indicating that the worker is duly paid.

Wages

- Non - Qualified Worker: 8.416,72 CRC per hour (US$16)
- Semi - Qualified Worker: 9.164,03 CRC per hour (US$17.2)
- Qualified Worker: 9.340,79 CRC per hour (US$18.60)
- High School level technicians: 303.137,69 CRC per month (US$608.12)
- Specialized Worker: 324.850,54 CRC per month (US$651.68)
- College technicians: 373.583,85 CRC per month (US$749.41)
- Bachelor's Degree: 403.484,51 CRC per month (US$809.39)
- *Licenciatura* Licensed Degree: 549.195,15 CRC per month (US$1101,69)

Types of Business Structures

- General Partnership (*Sociedad en Nombre Colectivo)*
- Limited Liability Company (*Sociedad de Resposibilidad Limitada)*

- Limited Partnership (*Sociedad en Comandita)*
- Limited Company/ Corporation (Sociedad Anonima)

General Bank Requirements for Individuals:

- Copy of your passport or residency card
- Reference letter from your current bank.
- Reference letter from account holder (some banks only)
- Tax return (some banks only)
- 12 months of banking statements (some banks only)
- Copy of your utility bill (required by all banks)
- Copy of the deed if ever you own any real estate property (some banks only)
- Know Your Customer Form (required by all banks)

PHOTO REFERENCES

Foreword Page Photo by user Ronny K via Pixabay.com,

https://pixabay.com/en/international-flag-costa-rica-2690996/

Page Photo by user BelaMarie via Pixabay.com,

https://pixabay.com/en/volcano-eruption-costa-rica-arenal-718277/

Page Photo by user davebaur via Pixabay.com,

https://pixabay.com/en/costa-rica-manuel-antonio-ocean-977048/

Page Photo by user Infinite Thought via Pixabay.com,

https://pixabay.com/en/water-fall-blue-water-nature-water-2355759/

Page Photo by user prohispano via Pixabay.com,

https://pixabay.com/en/happy-dance-costa-rica-honduras-2723487/

Page Photo by user Kristendawn via Pixabay.com,

https://pixabay.com/en/beach-sunset-coast-costa-rica-2580656/

Page Photo by user Infinite Thought via Pixabay.com,

https://pixabay.com/en/sunset-costa-rica-beach-nature-2355774/

Page Photo by user Jeremy 924 via Pixabay.com,

https://pixabay.com/en/quesadillas-costa-rica-food-quesadillas--2124910/Page Photo by user via Pixabay.com,

Page Photo by user Trevor Huxham via Flickr.com,

https://www.flickr.com/photos/ferrariguy90/5975801387/

Page Photo by user Ali Emino via Flickr.com,

https://www.flickr.com/photos/aliarda/5466725442/

Page Photo by user Speed of Life Tours via Flickr.com,

https://www.flickr.com/photos/speedoflifetours/9620872513/

Page Photo by user John Menard via Flickr.com,

https://www.flickr.com/photos/jmenard48/5700152638/

Page Photo by user Marv Gillibrand via Flickr.com,

https://www.flickr.com/photos/marv/357255767/

Page Photo by user MadriCR via Flickr.com,

https://www.flickr.com/photos/60167885@N04/16643470408/

Page Photo by user Terry Feuerborn via Flickr.com,

https://www.flickr.com/photos/travfotos/4616528215/

Page Photo by user GothPhil via Flickr.com,

https://www.flickr.com/photos/phil_p/1447252107/

Page Photo by user Haphazard Traveler via Flickr.com,

https://www.flickr.com/photos/davidambrocik/4491602914/

Page Photo by user UGA College of Ag & Environmental Science via Flickr.com,

https://www.flickr.com/photos/ugacommunications/1699797
0262/

Page Photo by user KFlotography via Flickr.com,

https://www.flickr.com/photos/keithaus/269552961/

Page Photo by user Trevor Huxham via Flickr.com,

https://www.flickr.com/photos/ferrariguy90/5976360010/in/photostream/

Page Photo by user Coral Blanche Hummer via Flickr.com,

https://www.flickr.com/photos/63527238@N03/7685731848/

Page Photo by user Penn State via Flickr.com,

https://www.flickr.com/photos/pennstatelive/16475582636/

Page Photo by user Marv Gillibrand via Flickr.com,

https://www.flickr.com/photos/marv/357255018/

Page Photo by user Maria Michelle via Pixabay.com,

https://pixabay.com/en/costa-rica-beach-outdoor-green-318914/

REFERENCES

Costa Rica History Timeline – WorldAtlas.com

https://www.worldatlas.com/webimage/countrys/namerica/camerica/costarica/crtimeln.htm

Costa Rica for Expats – MontezumaBeach.com

http://www.montezumabeach.com/costa-rica-for-expats/

COSTA RICA: Provinces and Urban Areas – CityPopulation.de

https://www.citypopulation.de/CostaRica-UA.html

Costa Rica Destinations – GoVisitCostaRica.com

https://www.govisitcostarica.com/regions.asp

Costa Rica 101: Fast Facts – VivaCostaRica.com

http://www.vivacostarica.com/costa-rica-information/costa-rica-facts.html

Costa Rica – WikiTravel.org

https://wikitravel.org/en/Costa_Rica

Customs & Etiquette - CostaRica.com

https://www.costarica.com/culture/customs-etiquette

Customs and etiquette: The Costa Rican way of life – JustLanded.com

https://www.justlanded.com/english/Costa-Rica/Costa-Rica-Guide/Culture/Customs-and-etiquette

Visas & Permits – JustLanded.com

https://www.justlanded.com/english/Costa-Rica/Visas-Permits

Costa Rica Immigration and Residency Summary – CostaRicaLaw.com

https://costaricalaw.com/costa-rica-legal-topics/immigration-and-residency/residency-general-information-and-summary/

The Truth about Living in Costa Rica: The Good, the Bad, and the Muddy – VivaTropical.com

https://vivatropical.com/costa-rica/living-in-costa-rica

Cities & Towns – VacationCostaRica.com

https://www.vacationscostarica.com/travel-guide/cities-towns/

Cost Of Living – CostaRica.com

https://www.costarica.com/relocation/cost-of-living

Cost of Living in Costa Rica – Numbeo.com

https://www.numbeo.com/cost-of-living/country_result.jsp?country=Costa+Rica

Where to Live in San José, Costa Rica – TripSavvy.com

https://www.tripsavvy.com/live-in-san-jose-costa-rica-1490191

Rent before you buy a home in Costa Rica? - American-European.net

https://www.american-european.net/costa-rica-real-estate-blog/costa-rica-real-estate-topics/rent-before-you-buy-a-home-in-costa-rica/

The 19-step Costa Rica real estate guide for foreign buyers - Ticotimes.net

http://www.ticotimes.net/realestate/the-19-step-costa-rica-real-estate-guide-for-foreign-buyers

Cell Phones - Costarica.com

https://www.costarica.com/relocation/cell-phones/

Everything about utilities in Costa Rica - Godutchrealty.com

https://www.godutchrealty.com/costa-rica-real-estate-blog/costa-rica-utilities/everything-about-utilities-in-costa-rica/

Costa Rica Guide - Jobs – JustLanded.com

https://www.justlanded.com/english/Costa-Rica/Jobs

Work Permits: When and how to apply for them – JustLanded.com

https://www.justlanded.com/english/Costa-Rica/Costa-Rica-Guide/Jobs/Work-Permits

Working in Costa Rica: Working hours, salaries and labor regulations – JustLanded.com

https://www.justlanded.com/english/Costa-Rica/Costa-Rica-Guide/Jobs/Working-in-Costa-Rica

Costa Rica: Expat Experiences – ExpatFocus.com

http://www.expatfocus.com/c/aid=3892/articles/costa-rica/setting-up-your-own-business-in-costa-rica-heres-what-you-need-to-know/

Lifestyle Feature – Raising a Child in Costa Rica - Howlermag.com

http://howlermag.com/2017/09/lifestyle-feature-raising-child-costa-rica/

Moving to Costa Rica with Children - Sendmesouth.com

http://sendmesouth.com/moving-to-costa-rica-with-children/

Costa Rica - Education and Schools – ExpatFocus.com

http://www.expatfocus.com/expatriate-costa-rica-education-schools

Tax Guide for US Expats Living in Costa Rica - USofaExpatTax.com

https://usofaexpattax.com/wordpress/2018/01/18/tax-guide-us-expats-living-costa-rica/

Opening a Bank Account in Costa Rica – CostaRicaLaw.com

https://costaricalaw.com/costa-rica-legal-topics/banking-laws-and-regulations/opening-a-bank-account-in-costa-rica/

Medical Costs in Costa Rica: A Brief Comparison to the U.S. - WeExpats.com

https://www.weexpats.com/medical-costs-in-costa-rica-a-brief-comparison-to-the-us/

A Healthcare Guide for Expat Retirees In Costa Rica - ExpatFocus.com

https://www.expatfocus.com/c/aid=4019/articles/costa-rica/a-healthcare-guide-for-expat-retirees-in-costa-rica/

Healthcare in Costa Rica - ExpatArrivals.com/

http://www.expatarrivals.com/costa-rica/healthcare-in-costa-rica

Costa Rica Movers Checklist - TheRealCostaRica.com

http://www.therealcostarica.com/moving_to_costa_rica/moving_checklist.html

The Joys of Retiring in Costa Rica - InternationalLiving.com

https://internationalliving.com/countries/costa-rica/retire/

Moving Timeline and Checklist – Costa Rica - Information.com/

http://costarica-information.com/about-costa-rica/economy/economic-sectors-industries/real-estate/real-estate-general/moving-to-costa-rica/moving-import/moving-timeline-and-checklist

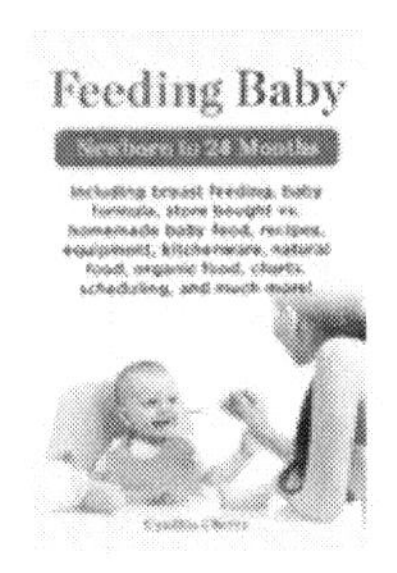

Feeding Baby
Cynthia Cherry
978-1941070000

Axolotl
Lolly Brown
978-0989658430

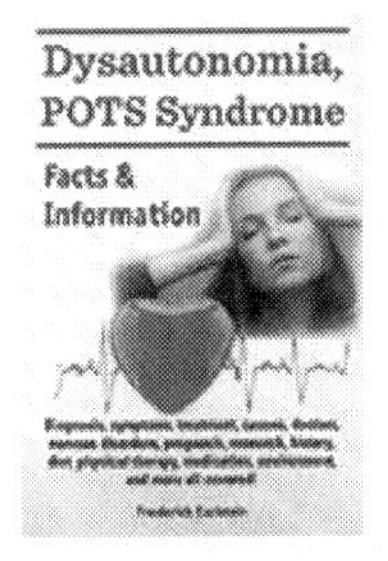

Dysautonomia, POTS Syndrome
Frederick Earlstein
978-0989658485

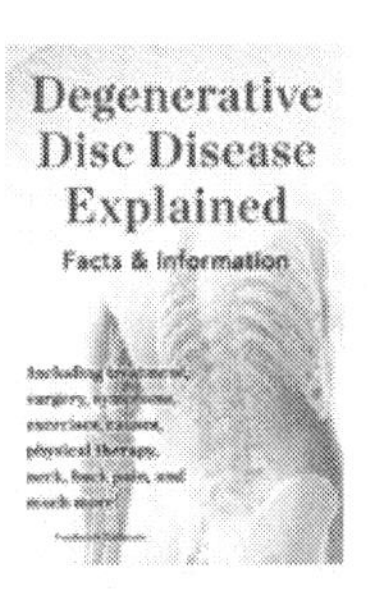

Degenerative Disc Disease Explained
Frederick Earlstein
978-0989658485

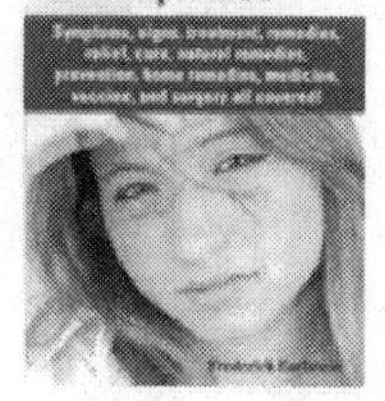

Sinusitis, Hay Fever,
Allergic Rhinitis Explained
Frederick Earlstein
978-1941070024

Wicca
Riley Star
978-1941070130

Zombie Apocalypse
Rex Cutty
978-1941070154

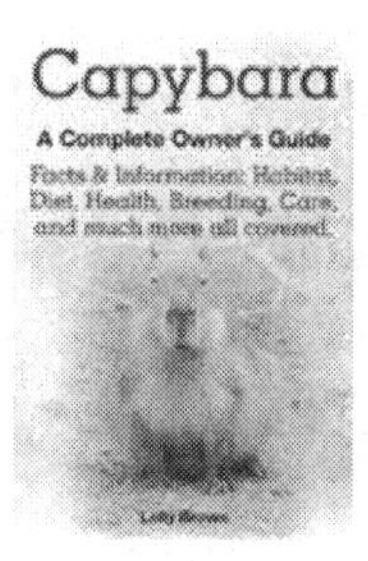

Capybara
Lolly Brown
978-1941070062

Eels As Pets
Lolly Brown
978-1941070167

Scabies and Lice Explained
Frederick Earlstein
978-1941070017

Saltwater Fish As Pets
Lolly Brown
978-0989658461

Torticollis Explained
Frederick Earlstein
978-1941070055

Kennel Cough
Lolly Brown
978-0989658409

Physiotherapist, Physical Therapist
Christopher Wright
978-0989658492

Rats, Mice, and Dormice As Pets
Lolly Brown
978-1941070079

Wallaby and Wallaroo Care
Lolly Brown
978-1941070031

Bodybuilding Supplements
Explained
Jon Shelton
978-1941070239

Demonology
Riley Star
978-19401070314

Pigeon Racing
Lolly Brown
978-1941070307

Dwarf Hamster
Lolly Brown
978-1941070390

Cryptozoology
Rex Cutty
978-1941070406

Eye Strain
Frederick Earlstein
978-1941070369

Inez The Miniature Elephant
Asher Ray
978-1941070353

Vampire Apocalypse
Rex Cutty
978-1941070321

Made in United States
Troutdale, OR
10/27/2024